Business for Doctors

How to Set Up and Run a Medical Practice

Danny Allen

Cartoon and cover design by Robbie Mills

Copyright © 2014 Danny Allen

ISBN-13: 978-1499658071
ISBN-10: 1499658079

All Rights Reserved. No part of this publication may be reproduced in any form or by any means, including scanning, photocopying, or otherwise without prior written permission of the copyright holder.

Disclaimer and Terms of Use: The Author and Publisher has strived to be as accurate and complete as possible in the creation of this book, notwithstanding the fact that she does not warrant or represent at any time that the contents within are accurate due to the rapidly changing nature of the Internet. While all attempts have been made to verify information provided in this publication, the Author and Publisher assumes no responsibility for errors, omissions, or contrary interpretation of the subject matter herein. Any perceived slights of specific persons, peoples, or organisations are unintentional. In practical advice books, like anything else in life, there are no guarantees of income made. Readers are cautioned to rely on their own judgment about their individual circumstances to act accordingly. This book is not intended for use as a source of legal, business, accounting or financial advice. All readers are advised to seek services of competent professionals in the legal, business, accounting, and finance fields.

Dedication

This book is dedicated to the memory of

Nicky Spreull

Nurse and friend

Other books by Danny Allen

We Need It By Next Thursday – The Joys of Writing Psychiatric Reports 2nd Edition 2014

Do You Know a Good Expert? - Lawyers Tell Psychiatrists What They Want 2nd Edition (Editor) 2014

It's a Shrinking Business – How to Run a Psychiatric Practice 2014

Contents

Foreword 7

Introduction 9

Chapter 1 - What will I do? 15

Chapter 2 - Setting up 25

Chapter 3 - The business plan 33

Chapter 4 - Marketing yourself 45

Chapter 5 - Legal and professional matters 55

Chapter 6 - Creating time 61

Chapter 7 – Working and being contactable 67

Chapter 8 – Using your own premises 73

Chapter 9 - Getting paid 83

Chapter 10 - Employing people 93

Chapter 11 - Keeping going 103

Chapter 12 - Expanding 111

Chapter 13 - Succession planning 119

Chapter 14 - Putting it into practice 125

Acknowledgements 141

About the author 143

Bibliography 145

Webography 147

Index 149

Business for Medics

Foreword

When Danny Allen asked me to write the foreword for this book, it was an honour and a privilege; an honour because the subject is one about which he is so well informed, and a privilege to be able to put in writing some thoughts about an old friend. Danny and I first met in 1974, when we started together as students at The Middlesex Hospital Medical School. It was immediately clear that he was unusual and as I got to know him better over the years this became clearer to me. He was always one of the most enquiring, analytical and organised people I knew. In his junior doctor days he tried his hand at several specialties, before finally training in his chosen specialty, so he would again be unusual, with more varied clinical experience than many in psychiatry. NHS practice occupies most of the time and energy for most hospital doctors, at least in their initial years, with private practice just being some icing on the cake. "If a job is worth doing, it's worth doing well", and if you are contemplating working in the independent sector, doing the job well means much more than simply doing a good job clinically. Medical training, particularly in hospital medicine, leaves most doctors without any idea of what it takes to be successful in business, but independent practice is exactly that, a business. Danny's detailed analytical approach has given him more insight into and awareness of the mundane but essential details necessary to organise oneself as an independent practitioner, while his organised mind has allowed him to set out these details in a clear and methodical manner in this book. He has lectured on this topic to many audiences, and this book reflects that experience, both in content and in the easy manner in which the material is communicated. I can vouch for most of the advice he offers, but I have had to learn this by trial and error, and a modicum of luck. When I first started, senior colleagues gave me some advice in an informal and anecdotal way; how much easier it would have been if I had read this book at the start of my consultant career. If you are a consultant starting out in private practice, buy this book; it is an investment which, literally, will pay dividends. Having read the book, you will realise that it is a tax-deductible item, which effectively means you are getting it at approximately 40% discount! If you are an experienced consultant with an established private practice, you will probably find a few useful nuggets, or alternatively take a newly-appointed junior colleague under your wing and start by buying this book for them.

Steve Krikler
Consultant Orthopaedic Surgeon

Introduction

Some doctors think that all they have to do, in order to go into private or medico-legal practice, is to show willing and charge money. The truth, unsurprisingly, is much more complex. For a number of years now I have been going up and down the country, giving short talks and whole day workshops on how doctors should run their businesses and I thought it was about time that I put this into writing, to open it up to a bigger audience.

This book draws on over twenty years' of experience; most of it found out either along the way or by making mistakes. Making mistakes is inevitable if you are making sufficient decisions - wise words from Pete Sudbury, my sometime medical director - but some mistakes can be too costly to contemplate and I heard quite a few horror stories from people in workshops, making me think that doctors really should learn a few things before they consider selling their services.

The fact that you have bought (or borrowed) this book suggests a certain degree of insight; others all too frequently carry on blithely, unaware that what they are doing is unlawful. So far I have yet to hear of a doctor being prosecuted for a failure to have employer's liability insurance, but one often hears of doctors pursued by HMRC (Her Majesty's Revenue and Customs) for failure to pay sufficient tax and it is inevitable that, where this crosses the threshold for criminal prosecution, these doctors will find themselves referred to the GMC (General Medical Council).

In this book I hope you will not only learn about the basics of setting up a business, but also some of the 'tricks of the trade'. Similarly it is important that you are aware of some of the common pitfalls, particularly in those circumstances where you are in real danger of breaking the law if you do not know what you are doing. In my estimation, private practice and medico-legal work should be pleasurable, lawful and profitable; all three matter, more or less equally.

Another important issue, for UK doctors, is that the vast majority of us work in the NHS and whilst some may only start a practice on retirement, many more will want to run one in parallel. Indeed, even if you are planning to start after retirement, you will soon gather, on reading this book, that this is not something you should contemplate without a certain amount of planning, so if you are looking for a smooth transition from NHS to private practice, you may well be advised to start whilst you are still employed. Thus I will spend some time talking about how the rules governing NHS contracts in England, at least as they pertain to working privately.

So what can you expect from this book? Well, by the time you have finished it you should be in a good position to start your practice on a sound basis. First and foremost, you will have recognised that you are going into business. This may sound totally daft, but my experience suggests that this is not really something which most doctors think about. They think they are doing a bit of doctoring and that the business aspects are for someone else. That 'someone' may be the clinic they are in or the hospital whose consulting rooms they rent – just not them!

Like most other things in medicine it pays to 'read around' your subject. By having a working understanding of the laws and conventions which surround the world of business, you will be in a much better position to think of the things you need to be considering, even if they are new – and new rules are promulgated with monotonous regularity – so that even if everything you read here is not 100% up to date (and how could it be) you will know who to ask to find out the up to date situation. So, by the end of this book, I hope you will be able to:

- Understand why slipping your NHS secretary a tenner for typing a report is unlawful
- Know how to negotiate space for your practice in your job plan
- Realise that an accountant is worth their weight in gold
- Be able to confidently issue tax compliant invoices.
- Have a good understanding of your responsibilities in the business world
- Know how to write a business plan
- Understand your extra professional responsibilities
- Make sure you train appropriately for your role
- Keep appropriate records
- Make sure you have a mentor or supervisor
- Always be ethical
- Create time to perform your role
- Be open with your employer
- Choose your workplace carefully
- Use modern tools to make yourself more available
- Understand how to employ people legally and ethically
- Use an outsourced payroll function

- Maintain good relationships with your customers
- Make sure you get paid
- Consider how to work with others
- Understand that your business has a value
- Network to get referrals/instructions
- Manage your time and delegate

I hope you enjoy reading this book and benefit from the information in contains. I apologise in advance for any inaccuracies. I have done my best to avoid them but in making the decision to write the book, I have inevitably opened myself up to the possibility that the odd one will slip in!

Business for Medics

Chapter 1 - What will I do?

Forgive me for putting this chapter in the book. If you know exactly what you are going to do and how you will do it, you may move straight to chapter 2. However, my experience of talking to people shows that doctors sometimes only have a very vague idea about what they want to do and, furthermore, how they might go about it. What am I talking about? Well, for example you may be a jobbing surgeon and think you want to do some private practice. However when you come to set up you realise that you rather like operating on people with some esoteric condition only your Trust specialises in but that private practice does not enable you to see people with this – possibly because your Trust has cornered the market and, even if they are referred, you lack the necessary team structure in your private hospital to deal with these patients effectively.

Alternatively you might want nothing to do with this in your private practice, considering that you want a complete change from what you do in the NHS. But you may not get referred many patients. So, if you are thinking of seeing private patients you may want to think of going into a niche area. Obviously this depends hugely on what area of medicine you are in

For doctors who like the idea of medico-legal work, they may think this is something they can just go straight into, but then find themselves embarrassed because they do not know how to compile a report, in particular because they do not know the rules which apply to their chosen field.

<u>Private practice</u>

Many psychiatrists run exclusively medico-legal practices (about which, more below), so deciding to see private patients is tantamount to making a choice – of course there is absolutely no reason why you should not do both but it is as well to think these things through because all choices have implications. First and foremost, as you will find out in Chapter 7, is the issue of where you can see patients. You are definitely constrained as to planning permission and, if you do no **NHS** practice, CQC (Care Quality Commission) rules and therefore, if you do not want to see that many patients, you may well decide that your best option is to get practising privileges at a local private hospital for this purpose.

However, for the purposes of this section, I shall assume that you are very keen on seeing private patients. The first thing to consider is the likely 'market'. There are no real shortcuts. You may need to ask a lot of people, GPs, colleagues etc. and even then you may be none the wiser. At the end of the day you may just need to 'dip your toe in the water'. But this means that you cannot (unless you have lots of money saved) expend vast quantities of money on premises or even staff. Hence renting rooms of one sort or another is probably your best option.

Private practice depends, inevitably, on money. This money will come either straight out of the pockets of your patients or from private insurance. In either case, unless you happen to live in a community of lottery winners and landed gentry, this will depend on people being in employment - and a lot less will be in a recession. So being aware of external financial realities is probably as important as knowing who you want to be treating.

So, of course you can be a 'broad-spectrum' doctor, but I suggest that it can be helpful to make known the areas of practice in which you have an 'interest', even if these are only those areas in which you think people will most need help – e.g. eczema if you are a dermatologist. Taking things a stage further, how about thinking about what is missing from the

NHS? What do people (GPs and patients) ask for but get denied? Obvious answers might include things like minor surgery.

Giving some thought to such matters enables you to plan ahead and, where appropriate, train for your role. I would suggest that, if you want to invest in your future private practice, a two day training course on some treatment modality not used by the NHS may be a better use of money, and, as you will discover in the next chapter, totally tax deductible, than renting medical chambers with no certainty of work.

Giving some thought to what you might like to do (and even training for the role) is only the beginning though, because some roles require you to 'partner' with others and though this may seem simple in theory my experience is that this is the point at which most schemes fall down. I have had numerous meetings with people who have brilliant ideas for 'services' but who do not have either the 'staying power' or the drive to make them come to fruition. These things are not for the faint-hearted, yet the concept of running a 'service' as opposed to just having a practice is very attractive, not only to the practitioners but also to patients and referrers. Well-run services should be able to both inspire confidence and deliver the goods but they take quite a lot of sustained effort to set up.

Medico-legal work

In certain specialties, notably general practice, A & E, orthopaedics and psychiatry, there is a lot of medico-legal work to be had but, these days, unlike 'when I were a lad' one would be well-advised to prepare and train carefully for the role. Not that I am trying to put anyone off. On the contrary I believe it to be a very fulfilling role and one which I would encourage any young doctor (and maybe even a few old ones) to get into. Just make sure you don't try to run before you can walk.

There are many courses, not least those run by Bond Solon, which exist to teach doctors about medico-legal work. At the point of writing there is no formal 'qualification' for being an expert, but there is a gentle pressure leading in this general direction and, in my book, wherever this is the case, it pays to get ahead of the game, even were it not a good idea in its own right.

At the very least it is as well to be aware that there are rules governing the three main jurisdictions, civil, criminal and family and to go looking for the one pertaining to your field(s). These rules require certain wording on reports and, if you fail to include this, you are going to look like a rank amateur. Far better, then, to invest some money in going on a course introducing you to report-writing. If you can find someone who already does this sort of work, why not approach them for some support and mentoring? Most of us are only too keen to help colleagues. For most specialties it is in the civil arena – personal injury and clinical negligence – that they will find most work. Psychiatrists have a broader choice.

The obvious place to start is with personal injury cases involving road traffic accidents. Most of these are handled by agencies, so you can look for agencies active at the time you read this book. I use this phrase advisedly because these companies have a nasty habit of going out of business without so much as a 'by your leave'. It pays to check them out and it pays to make sure you get a formal contractual agreement as to when you will be paid – and if you are not, to seriously consider suing them for any money owing before they go bankrupt. More of this below.

Other streams of work

What else might doctors do? Well they may teach, they may write (including books!) and they may become appraisers (of colleagues for revalidation purposes – a growing career choice!). Some of these roles, at least, are clearly paid work but differ from pure employment by the discretion associated with the choice of working hours. Hence they fit well into a 'portfolio career'. Some colleagues feel very strongly that 'time is money' and demand payment for anything. You will have to decide where you sit on the spectrum. I have accepted money for lecturing when it is offered, for example, but I don't always insist on it.

By the way, don't expect to make much (if any) money from writing books! Unless you are a great academic (in which case still don't expect to be able to retire on the proceeds) you are likely, these days, to spend a small amount self-publishing, then struggle to recoup your costs. But it is really jolly good fun and you should not be put off if you feel the urge. It is great for filling in those gaps where work is slack, patients or clients don't show or that week between Xmas and New Year when everything closes down and you want to get away from the in-laws!

Some doctors, particularly those who have left the NHS, like to combine self-employment with a part-time job. This is often an excellent option. Such jobs are sometimes available within the NHS to people after retirement; as a basic rule of thumb for people under 60 (where these rules apply) you can work for up to 2 days - 4PAs (professional activities) a week without a decrement in your pension. However, please do not *rely* on this book − rules change and you must always check these things with your pension provider. If you are lucky enough to get even one PA's work then (at the point of writing) you are absolved from having to register with the CQC for your private practice (there is more about this in Chapters 7 and 11). Again rules change so you must check the up to date situation. It depends on your specialty but all sorts of jobs exist and a regular scan of the BMJ careers pages or the like will keep you informed. You may be asked to become a (non-executive) director of a charity involved with some area of medical practice. If you are tempted in this direction I would also advise you to train appropriately for the role − the Institute of Directors does some very good courses.

In this chapter we have looked at some of the choices available to doctors who want to go into practice. The main two are private (medical) practice and medico-legal practice, and many will choose to do both together. Having the ability to diversify is important as external constraints may influence what is available at any point in time.

Business for Medics

Chapter 2 - Setting up

In this chapter we will look at the basics of running a business – as this is what you are doing if you are working for money on your own account. The biggest mistake made by doctors is to not take this aspect of work seriously. It matters because there are certain laws which govern business behaviour and you ignore them at your peril.

Thinking about things before you spring into action

Most doctors, including even myself, will do some work for money before setting up as a business. The reason for this is obvious. Sometimes in life things creep up on us and catch us unawares. In my case I started a forensic psychiatry job and was taught how to write reports. It was, of course, normal practice to ask for payment for these reports which had to be typed by someone and thus we were 'instructed' to pay the secretaries who typed them. For others, you might find yourself filling in 'crem forms'. The first thing to bear in mind is that, as long as you are simply being paid for something, you will remain on the right side of the law as long as you declare your earnings. However this is likely not to be the case once you pay someone else.

Also, the law allows you some leeway to register as self-employed after you have started earning money. The longer you leave it, though, the more advisable it is to get expert advice – certainly it is wise to do so if more than a year has passed. The key reason and, indeed, the main issue, which I hope you will appreciate as you read on, is that you are the loser if you simply declare your earnings. The taxman will be delighted to take 40% of everything you declare, no questions asked. The law allows you to keep some of this but, in order to do this you need to be accepted as a self-employed person. Secondly, as you will learn, double taxation in 'year one' is better done whilst you are still earning a pittance.

So, although many people find themselves being asked to do work before they have considered 'setting up', the sooner you do this the better and ideally you should do this, at your leisure, before you are earning 'serious money'. But there is no harm in being prepared and declaring no income for a year or two. In the 'real world' many businesses (plan to) make losses in their first few years' trading anyway so a zero balance is absolutely fine and indeed you may think of some things you need to buy ahead of the time when you will earn money in order for you to do your work. What about an item of necessary equipment, for instance?

The other issue to consider is the extent to which you want to 'go it alone'. I remembering going round to my friend's house (the very one who has written the foreword to this book) when I was a medical student and his father, who by this time was a judge, gave me some sage advice: "Get an accountant before you need one". I would add that this accountant should be a good one - ask around amongst those who are well informed. Whilst this is advice I commend to you, many of the steps I will outline below you can do alone and may want to in the early days. That said, having the structure of having to report to an accountant is a good discipline and ultimately 'protective' against the ravages of the taxman - and you won't have to pay for the things you do yourself. 'Throwing' all your receipts at the accountant and expecting him or her to sort out your tax return is going to work out a hell of a lot more expensive - and probably not worth your while - compared with presenting him or her with a spreadsheet summarising your incomings and outgoings.

Starting a business

Firstly you need to register with HMRC as a business. Forms can easily be found online and you can do this retrospectively within the first year. You will need a name – even if it is as simple as Dr Bloggs Medical Practice.

You need to be aware that you will be taxed double in your first year (you get this back when your business is wound up). This is an excellent reason for registering early – before you find this is too onerous. You need to decide on your accounting year. You can stick with the tax year but, if you are good at putting money aside, you may wish to consider one which finishes on, for example, April 30th. This means you have over a year to collect the money from your debtors before tax is due.

You also need to fill in an annual form to 'defer' national insurance contributions. This assumes you are already earning over the maximum contribution income with your employment. The term 'defer' actually means not paying any via your business because you have already paid it in your employment. If all this sounds complicated – get an accountant!

Running a business

You need to be 'business-like'. This means having some discipline in the way you conduct your affairs, like having a 'proper' invoicing system. You should have numbered sequential invoices, dated and signed by yourself or your representative. They should show a reliable trading address and give any information about the name of your business, particularly if they are issued under a trading name. They should state the nature of the service and when it was performed. You should have a way of collecting and recording what money you have collected. Cheap accounting systems are easy to come by but in the early days you can just use a numbered invoice system on an ordinary 'Word' document if you wish. Records have to be kept for at least 6 years in case HMRC audits your business.

The more you can do yourself, the less you need to pay an accountant for. At each stage of your expansion, think about whether it is cheaper to employ someone to do a task for you than to either spend your (relatively expensive) time or your accountant's possibly more expensive time. There is more information in Chapter 7 - about employing people.

From the start you need to get into the habit of documenting and keeping evidence of your expenses, to set off against your income; otherwise you will pay too much tax! So keep, in some sort of order, your receipts. Remember that anything associated with your business is fair game as can be parts of things you use for business. A list of categories is available on a standard self-employed tax return. Again you are best checking with an accountant who, in the early days at least, is likely to be able to offset the value of his or her fees with the money you can save!

Legal issues pertaining to business

The major issue in business (before you start employing people) is tax law. Unless you register as a business, and therefore get taxed under a self-employment regime, you only have two choices. The first is 'forget' to declare additional income. This is clearly unlawful and ultimately may be criminal. The second is to declare income as 'additional'. For very occasional amounts this may be fine but as you start earning more you will inevitably end up paying too much tax. This is because it is only by registering as a business/self-employed that you can claim expenses.

My advice is also to get a business account, to keep business earnings separate, with a deposit account to save for tax. In the event of any HMRC investigation will also demonstrate that you have kept a proper separation between business and personal finances meaning that there is less of a chance of the investigation 'bleeding' into other areas of your finances..

In this chapter we have covered the basics of business. Firstly setting up by registering with HMRC, secondly organising yourself along business-like lines, keeping all receipts and recording all transactions. The importance of having an accountant from a very early stage was emphasised, as was the danger, legally, of doing things improperly.

Chapter 3 - The business plan

In this chapter we will look at the concept of a business plan, what it is used for and when you might need one. We will go through the main headings a typical business plan may contain.

First, a confession. I drifted into business, making numerous mistakes along the way. By the time I wrote my first business plan I had been doing medico-legal work for over a decade. During the latter part of this period, I had started working with some colleagues, who joined me in my business. I then sat down with some colleagues, to set up a private practice, and it was only then that I was made aware of the need to have a business plan, as we wanted to pitch our idea to a local private hospital.

The second time I wrote a business plan was when a marketing agent got me to do this prior to building me a new website. And the third time was when I wanted to increase my overdraft with the bank. I was quite nervous about the last occasion but was actually praised for my creation!

However, a business plan can be quite a useful tool just for your own use, and it follows on neatly from thinking about what you want to do and how you need to do it, as discussed in the last two chapters. So, the choice is yours, there is certainly no legal need to have a plan, and if you start small, or work alongside your NHS job, you will survive just fine without one but since, one day, you may be called upon to produce one here are a few words about what it should contain.

Of course, as with everything else, do not rely solely on this book to guide you but think of it more as a starting point to further exploration. What I am about to demonstrate is, after all, just one possible way of doing things.

So, the first thing is to create a document which is entitled 'Business Plan for Dr Bloggs' Medical Practice, you then need to state the timescale it covers. Is it going to be like a Soviet 5-year plan or a more modest 1 or 2 year projection of what you see happening (or would like to happen)? Then write your name underneath and start the headings:

Introduction

This section should be written with the idea that the reader knows nothing about what you do: 'Mr Smith Orthopaedic

Practice' is a surgical practice which provides, assessment, diagnosis and follow up of children and adults referred from their general practitioner with problems affecting their bones and joints. It also provides surgical services (exploratory, reparative and revision operations) in conjunction with Dr Small anaesthetic practice and the Sloan Ranger Private Hospital.

Executive Summary

Like all good summaries, although this appears at the beginning for those too lazy to read the whole document, it should be written at the end, when you know what you have said!

My suggested subheadings for this section are as follows:

- Summary

- The market and business

- Core product offerings

- Revenues and profitability

- Management team

Yes, I know this all sounds a bit 'business-school, but the whole purpose of the exercise is to make you think about what you are doing from a business perspective. There is no point doing something if, for example, you are going to fail to make a profit because you had not considered realistically what your expenses might be.

Terms like 'core product offerings' could be substituted, if this feels too much like a hardware store for your liking, but you do need to think what it is you are offering the public which is likely to make money – and of which there is enough of in the general population to ensure a steady flow of referrals eventually.

Business Mission

Yes, this is the good old 'mission statement' by another name, but it does not have to be corny. It may make you think though – if only about how you don't want to overstep the mark and upset the GMC. You cannot make wild or unreasonable claims for what you want to do. Here is mine for my medico-legal business:

> Our mission is to be a quality provider of medico-legal services, primarily in the south of England.
>
> To do this we need to find and develop new associates who have a proven track record and get them to work with us as well as increasing the number and breadth of instructions received centrally.
>
> We want to deliberately target not only existing core business streams but to ensure that we develop all of the eight available streams to the best of our ability. We should also keep a look out for other business ventures which will complement our existing work.
>
> We will succeed because we will adopt proven marketing techniques and implement rigorous feedback to ensure we only target profitable revenue streams.

So, only slightly grandiose, then!

Company ownership/location

This should be quite straightforward, but is part of probity. You do need to be transparent, if your (life) partner is also a 'sleeping partner' in the business.

This refers to someone who shares the tax bill (and therefore lessens your joint tax liability) but does not necessarily contribute to the running of the business (more about this in chapter 9).

External analysis

This is an attempt at some evidence-based business and my suggested headings are:

- The economy & business environment
- Target customers/market dynamics
- Competition (including a competitor grid)
- Market size

Internal analysis

This is a look at what you do (or hope to do) within your business. So the main headings are:

- Our products and services
- Marketing

Under the first heading you can list what you provide. If you think about professionals who practise privately, like dentists, you will consider that they offer more than just their obvious core dental skills, dental hygienists are an important service and they also can sell dental products at reception. Don't pooh-pooh this approach, you may find a profitable side-line relevant to your specialty. For example our office manager is a trained forensic 'hair-cutter' for the purposes of hair-strand testing for drugs and alcohol, a service we provide in conjunction with our core medico-legal work, using an external company. We also can take blood for testing, something we charge extra for.

Here are some possible marketing techniques doctors can use over and above putting adverts into local magazines and the like:

- Website
- App
- Webinars
- Talks
- Books
- Articles
- Direct personal conversations

More about this in Chapter 4.

SWOT analysis

Just in case you have got this far in life without encountering this term, the acronym stands for:

- Strengths
- Weaknesses
- Opportunities
- Threats

This is not just an opportunity to be trendy. Think hard about what your strengths really are, and not just those core ones which make you a surgeon or physician. Also don't just think about yourself. Can you work with others to improve the service you offer? I work with a psychiatric nurse. Can you work with an audiologist, a diabetic nurse?

Think about what your weaknesses are; this refers not only to your own issues but to your location or the size of your premises.

Conversely what opportunities lie ahead? Is Dr Ashurst going to be retiring soon? Perhaps he would like to have a young colleague to pass all his patients to?

And lastly what threats are there about. Is your best friend from your surgical rotation about to set up practice in the next town? Is there another recession on the way? Is the local source of employment about to go bust?

Strategies

This section should look at your pricing strategy using best available information. Once you are already in practice you can look at your sales summary to see if pricing can be tweaked to improve your sales. I know this sounds very 'business-like' and feels as if it has nothing to do with the practice of medicine, but this book is about business! You may have set your prices by putting a finger in the wind. Alternatively you may argue that you have little choice what you charge, given the tight hold of the insurance companies. Fine – at least you have thought about it. But there may be areas which you can expand upon and which may subsidise these relatively inflexible items.

It may help you to include, in this section, a plan for what you propose doing to increase business over the next 12 months. And, if you are a medium size organisation like my own with in excess of twenty 'players' it helps to explain the relationships and how governance works.

Marketing Plan

You mean you don't have one already? This is your opportunity to think of some ideas. Perhaps, when you think about marketing you think about more 'above the line' activities such as TV, radio, posters and press. Most of these are not really for doctors are they? How about some of these 'below the line' ideas though:

- Internet site
- Blogging

- Email marketing
- Press releases
- Social media
- Professional networking
- Promotional material
- Magazine marketing
- Video marketing
- Newsletter
- Database management
- Epubs/ebooks
- Word of mouth

More about this in the next chapter!

Finances

Ah, you were wondering when I would come to money. Well, at the start of your business, there may be little you can say about this, but it is always wise to consider the basic business costs you will undoubtedly have. You then need to earn sufficient money to cover these, before you make a profit. If you have savings you may need to 'put money into the business; to 'pump prime' it. This all needs to go into this section.

In this chapter we have looked at one way of producing a business plan, the main headings it should contain and we have also considered when you might want or need to have such a tool.

Chapter 4 - Marketing yourself

In this chapter we will think about how you can make people aware of your existence, what you do and where you do it and look at some techniques for driving 'customers' in your general direction.

When I give talks on business I usually get one person who says something along these lines: "Doesn't the GMC forbid doctors from advertising". Now, I hope most readers will recognise that this concept is approximately thirty years out of date. The GMC, in its interim phase, did actually produce a brochure on this very topic but now you just need to read all their documents carefully to be aware of their general approach, which, I would argue, is eminently sensible and well-balanced.

In essence, what you are allowed to do, as a doctor, is to make known to the public and colleagues, what you do, what your special interests and experience are, how much you charge etc. What you are most definitely not allowed to do is to make claims which are untruthful, disparaging to others or suggest that you have special skills others don't have. So a simple statement about you yourself, your experience and your interests is fine. Here is the sort of thing I have in mind, taken and suitably anonymised from one of my colleagues:

- General Surgeon. Past Consultant Breast Surgeon at St Artefacts Hospital and Senior Lecturer at Clapham Medical School
- Past examiner at the Royal College of Specialists. Approved under some arcane rules known only to this specialty.

- Contributor to over 100 scientific papers, articles and books on breasts, more breasts and virtually nothing but the breast.

- Honorary Consultant at the Cathedral NHS Foundation Trust.

- Member of the Very Important Governmental Support Team.

- Awarded "Super Duper Team of the Year 2013" by the Royal College of Specialists.

On the other hand, if you look on the internet you will see some statements which are possibly in a slightly greyer area:

Mr X is one of the most senior collywobble-ologists practising in the UK. He has had more than Y years of clinical and academic experience during which time he has successfully diagnosed and treated patients from all over the world. He is particularly recognised for his diagnostic skills and his expertise in treating and managing problems across the entire collywobble spectrum.

I would definitely encourage you to veer towards the former and steer clear of the latter, because you never know where this will lead. If you have in your mind's eye, the panel at the Medical Practitioners Tribunal Service (MPTS) this will probably concentrate your mind: "So Mr X, there are maybe 192 countries in the world, can you give the panel evidence of all the patients you have seen from Bhutan in the last 5 years?" "And by the way, what exactly do you mean by 'successfully diagnosed and treated'?"

Doctors are also required to be honest and transparent, to show probity, to be fair and to always put their patients' best interests first. Whilst there is no requirement to publish, for example, your fees, neither should you be so loathe to give out any detail that you appear to have something to hide. So, having laid out the ground rules, what should you be doing?

A website

Having a website these days is pretty much 'de rigeur'. I think that people tend to be a little suspicious of you if you don't have a web presence these days, but it is important to recognise what it is for. I would suggest that only a limited number of solicitors will choose you because of your medico-legal website (or the medico-legal section of your unitary website). However, I believe that patients do choose doctors from websites and then ask their GPs to refer them. This, anyway, is the evidence from our experience and is clearly different to the 'old days' when patients would expect their GPs to choose the expert. Not that this never happens but you will lose out without a website.

So, where to start? To make all this happen my advice is to find yourself a good designer *not*, primarily, a web/technical person – the latter, in my experience, is putting the cart before the horse. Once you have a good design, all the technical stuff should follow (good designers will work with 'techies'). This includes the 'statutory stuff' like making sure there is a notice about cookies, as well as the important practical stuff like making sure the website is adapted for smart phones and is easily changeable by yourself in the future. A website should be kept up to date and its primary purpose is to 'drive' people towards contacting you. It is also a great opportunity for you to put yourself across to a wider audience. When you do this, be aware that you have to put the name of your business on the website. This is especially important if you are using a trading name as the headline of the website – e.g. your business name is actually Dr Jones Paediatric Practice but you trade as 'Kids Are Us'. Somewhere at the bottom of the front page of the website should be something along the lines of "Kids Are Us is a trading name of Dr Jones Paediatric Practice'

Search engine optimisation is all the rage. What this means is that the search engine will find your website because it has something new on it. It is also cheaper than paying for this service (through Google AdWords for example). One easy way of doing this is to get a blog on your website (and remember to write something in it – or get someone else to submit articles - regularly. Believe me this is really easier said than done though!

Social Media

Probably all of us use social media – for social purposes. This is about creating a business persona – which may be 'you' or your business. Different platforms allow different things and there are several ways to skin a cat. For example you can register yourself on LinkedIn and you can also create an entity which is your business name and (if you have one) logo.

Facebook allows you to create business pages and Twitter lets you use several manifestations. Similarly Google+. Use social media both to contact colleagues and to 'push' them towards your website and your business. Again doing this regularly is easier said than done, so you may want to use 'meta' providers such as HootSuite or Buffer to 'broadcast' on multiple platforms. Using their tools to 'broadcast' articles of interest to your specialty which you search for or find serendipitously on the web is a cheap and cheerful way of doing this – and, if you have the time, you can add brief comments of your own.

Don't expect miracles from this technique – it is a slow 'drip-drip' which eventually gets the message though and it can be difficult to know if it is working – you need to persist at a rate you can stomach!

Entries in directories and registers

If you do medico-legal work it may be worth being in one or two expert witness directories, so people can find you if they have incomplete details. However, make sure you have a system for monitoring what brings people to you, so you can work out if these are really of any use. My experience suggests they are probably not terribly helpful in the bigger scheme of things and can cost quite a lot of money year on year (though this is always tax deductible!).

There are also some private practice equivalents and you can find draft ones in existence on sites like Dr Foster, which you can update and/or correct. You can also encourage patients to comment about you at 'I Want Great Care' (see Webography)

Talking

Giving talks to GPs or solicitors, giving lectures, teaching students etc. are clearly all good in their own right, but in the context of marketing can offer added opportunities. For example you should always take along some cards or promotional material (see below) and should always make sure you work into whatever you are saying something about how people can refer to you, how you can be contacted etc. If this goes against the grain at first – get used to it! It will soon become second nature!

Writing

Again, writing things is what we doctors do, articles, papers in learned journals, responses to queries all have a marketing angle which you can exploit without being overly blatant and irritating. You need to get your name about and you should not be shy about offering your services – for free- this is not a money-making exercise remember and buying conventional advertising will always be more expensive than your time and probably not as effective either.

Business Cards

Early on in your private or medico-legal career, get yourself several boxes of well-made and attractive business cards – preferably including a discreet logo which matches the one your designer created on your website. Hopefully that same designer can organise these for you. Then carry some with you *at all times*! You will never believe how difficult this is to do for most doctors, but business people do it all the time. You should have a very low threshold indeed for handing these out to all and sundry. Think of them as an adjunct to a handshake! Most will get binned but you just don't know who aunt is going to need a knee replacement or whose nephew needs a myringotomy.

Promotional materials

Given what I have said about the GMC you should not go mad on this one but if you offer certain specialist services or simply want to lay out your stall, there is nothing wrong with asking your designer to help you design leaflets and the like which can be made available to groups of people when you go around giving talks. As ever, they should be factual in content but as long as you stick to this mantra there is no reason at all why you should not say what you do. These can be information sheets with your contact details on or more holistic information about your practice. The only thing I would say is that posting these things out to multiple GPs, for example, can be very expensive and may not get past the receptionist's waste paper bin.

In this chapter, then, we have considered ways in which doctors can promote what they do to their prospective customers, whilst ensuring that they do not incur the wrath of the GMC. The primary methods are websites, social media, talking, writing, business cards and promotional materials.

Chapter 5 - Legal and professional matters

In this chapter we will look at your duties and responsibilities as a professional and specifically as a doctor.

Data

Anyone who handles data must be registered under the appropriate category with the Information Commissioner's Office. You can find details online. It is also good practice to tell patients or clients about how you will be using their data (for admin, letters to GPs and reports for example). A good place to give this information is in their appointment letter. Please note that this is not something you can leave to any hospital where you see patients or clients. These days they will normally expect you to provide evidence that you are registered as a data controller in your own right.

You also need, as a data controller, to make sure that the data you hold is held securely. There is no prescription for exactly how you should do this but you need to take common-sense reasonable precautions. For example, locked filing cabinets and password-protected computers should be the norm. If you transport notes in your car, a locked briefcase and not leaving it in the car whilst you pop to the pub are sensible precautions.

If you do need to send documents by email, you should encrypt them – and make sure the password is agreed other than by an email sent just after or just before to the same email address as the document (a common practice which has no security value if you think about it). A verbally agreed password is one possible solution. Another is to agree passwords by email sent from the putative receiver's email to the putative sender's, at a completely separate time in advance.

Better still, there are a number of 'platforms' for uploading documents to 'the cloud' which can be password-protected and many, such as Google Drive, offer free means for storing files securely (assuming this term has some meaning post-Snowden). Google Drive, in particular, has a useful function for connecting to Google Calendar so that files can be connected to client or patient appointments and other data.

The notes of adult patients need to be kept for 20 years at least and even longer for children. Medico-legal notes have to be kept for 6-10 years. Keeping them in perpetuity (in a scanned archive) is one sensible option (see the Webography for details).

Medical Defence

You need to make sure that you are signed up with a medical defence organisation and that the level of your cover is appropriate for the work you do. There will usually be some sort of tariff for both private and medico-legal work. If there is a change in the amount you earn (or are likely to earn that year) you must inform them; this is not something you should put off. I would also suggest that you develop a low threshold for ringing them up and seeking advice about anything with which you are unfamiliar or uncertain. Prevention is always better than cure. You can also write to them with information about issues you feel have the potential to 'blow up' even when nothing has happened and they can keep the information on file.

Insurance

You need to consider what insurance you need. We will deal with employees below but the sorts of things you need to be thinking about include insurance of any premises you own or rent and their contents as well as public liability insurance. If you already have health-related income protection insurance, remember to extend it to your independent practice – or maybe this is the time to get advice from an Independent Financial Advisor (IFA). A particularly useful type of insurance you may not have heard of (unless you have an accountant) is tax investigation insurance in case HMRC decide to audit you. However well organised you are, a tax audit is time consuming and, if you are insured, that time (and associated expense) can be your accountant's.

Training and Supervision

Just like any new role you need to train for what you do. Whilst this may not be so relevant for private practice, it is absolutely vital, these days, that if you want to do any medico-legal work whatsoever, you understand what jurisdiction you are working in and get appropriately trained. There are lots of courses on the internet; Bond Solon is one example of a company which specialises in this sort of course. You don't want to make a fool of yourself because you did not know that you needed to put a particular prescribed 'Statement of Truth' on your report, for example. There are separate sets of rules, these days, for each type of reports; for civil reports these are the Civil Procedure Rules (CPR) – you get the broad picture.

Continuing Professional Development (from a GMC viewpoint) needs to cover all aspects of your practice. In any case meeting a group of colleagues, for example to have a case-based discussion around medico-legal reports or patient-focussed problems is good practice. Finding a good mentor is also a good idea. Many people who have done this sort of work for years would be very willing to support you. Some charge; others don't – shop around.

In this chapter we covered the requirements all data handlers have to register with the Information Commissioner and to safeguard data. We looked at the specific responsibilities doctors have to be appropriately covered by their defence organisation, we considered what insurance one may need to take out and thought about the importance of appropriate training and supervision.

Business for Medics

Chapter 6 - Creating time

In this chapter we will look at the practicalities of setting up and running a practice at the same time as doing your NHS or other main role. We will consider the benefits of delegation and start thinking about how employing people to help you can assist in freeing up your time.

Job planning

There is a very clear structure for consultants to plan their job within the NHS. Sometimes job planning in the NHS is more often observed in the breach. It is tempting to just get on with your private or medico-legal practice and not say anything. However, at the very least, when a job-planning meeting is arranged by your employer, you need to be completely up-front about what you are doing as a failure to do so will lead to questions about your probity being raised.

The so-called 'new' contract (possibly soon to become 'old'), which virtually all consultants will now be on, has a specific requirement with regard to private practice for full time (10 PA) consultants. In order to work privately one has to 'offer' the Trust a session of (paid) extra work. Depending on your specialty, this may either be a legal fiction, or something to be taken quite seriously. Your medical director may actually want you to fulfil a specific role – but of course s/he may not necessarily wait until your job-planning meeting to inform you of this.

No such stipulation exists for medico-legal work but in both cases your manager has a legitimate interest in knowing something about what you do. There is no requirement for you to tell them how much you earn though many would love to know. A benign explanation of this thirst for knowledge would be that it is a proxy for how much time you spend. Better to tell them how much time you spend then!

A job plan has to be agreed, at the end of the day, so it is really by way of a negotiation, albeit one where the sides are not necessarily equally balanced. You should be looking for what you need, whilst bearing in mind the needs of your employer. Many Trusts are happy for their consultants to do, say, one or two medico-legal reports a week in Trust time, more so if you are a forensic psychiatrist. You are less likely to be allowed to do private work in Trust time so this, and in many cases medico-legal work too, needs to be done in evening and weekends, unless you can negotiate that your 10 PAs are not worked between Monday and Friday 9-5.

If you want to do your work in your Trust's premises you need to be clear that this is sanctioned by your manager – they may want paying – this is only to be expected but would be a deductible expense for your business. These things have to be discussed – avoidance can lead down the path of your probity being brought into question.

The important thing is to be open about what you do and everyone should be satisfied that you are not spending so much time and attention on this work that you are not able to give adequate attention to your Trust duties. Whilst the negotiation can, at times, be uncomfortable, you will sleep easier afterwards knowing that everything is above board.

Time management

If you are one of those people who is always punctual, can compartmentalise their lives and always manages to fit things in, skip to the next chapter. Everyone else read on! Still with us? – here goes:

If you have never been on a time management course, find one and do it! You may actually learn something If you are going to be doing three things at once (your day job, your personal life and your burgeoning private or medico-legal practice) you had better get used to juggling things. Of course some people are always going to be better at this than others but you can learn and you can improve.

The first thing to do is to create a particular time in the week when you can do this work and arrange things accordingly. This includes any room hire, childcare and support services such as secretarial support. Even if you are not at the stage where you will fill a weekly slot, it is as well that people know when it is, so try not to make yourself too available for other things at this time or it will soon be eroded.

One way of doing this is to use the time for other business related activities until you have people to see. Perhaps speaking to GPs or giving talks on your chosen niche specialty, maybe finding out which solicitors in your area need expert reports done.

Delegation

When you start you will have to do almost everything yourself. However very quickly you will realise the benefit of delegation. Unlike in the NHS where things are either given to you or not, in business you will have to buy or pay for them! Typing short letters and reports is fine but sooner or later you will want something more. Whatever you do, don't pay money to people to do things for you without reading the Chapter 7 - on employment - or you may all too easily find yourself breaking the law. In particular please don't fall into the trap of paying your NHS secretary (should you be lucky enough to still have one) to do your private or medico-legal work without understanding your legal responsibilities as an employer.

Clearly this does not mean, either, that you can ask them to work for free – or pass the work off as Trust work – this would clearly raise serious probity issues. Yet I mention it because we have probably all heard of both happening.

However, there are other things you may want to consider – voice transcription technology is continually improving and software is very affordable. It is not for everyone but many colleagues swear by it. Another aspect to consider is how people contact you. Of course if they ring you at your NHS office you cannot ignore them but you do need to consider the official way in which you should be contacted. If you do your work at a private hospital this may well be sorted, but if you work elsewhere or do medico-legal work you may like to explore other options. Clearly your mobile phone is one – but you do need to be a bit cautious as this could easily intrude into your NHS job and speaking to GPs about private patients (unless in an emergency) or solicitors about clients, during your ward rounds is going to be frowned upon. Answering services – a number of which you can find on the web - are certainly one solution to explore.

In this chapter we have looked at the importance of creating some protected time for you to do your private or medico-legal work. If you work in the NHS you must declare this in your job plan and in order to be effective you need to manage your time well. As things get busier you need to think about delegating activities to prevent work encroaching on personal and NHS time.

Chapter 7 – Working and being contactable

In this chapter we will look at where you can work from and the legal restrictions which may apply. We will also consider various virtual and non-geographical services which can aid you in setting up a business when you don't have much money to spend.

Location

Whether you are seeing private patients or writing medico-legal reports, the bottom line is that you need somewhere to see the people you are interviewing and this place needs to be clean, warm and present a sufficiently professional aura for people to feel confident in you as a doctor. So it is hardly surprising that many people will consider seeing people in their daytime place of work. As mentioned above this comes with several caveats, the most important of which is getting the permission of the Trust you work for. It is much more common for medico-legal reports where there are few constraints as to where people can be seen.

Although many people work in hospital settings where the Trust will have planning permission to see patients, some

Trust offices do not have such permission and clinical work is done in a different location. Whilst these offices might be acceptable for seeing clients for medico-legal reports they will not be acceptable for seeing patients.

In any case it is unlikely that you will be given permission to see private patients in Trust premises unless special arrangements have been made which are shared between the consultant body. These do exist – and there are sometimes cooperative ventures with private hospitals.

A common location for seeing private patients is a private hospital. You can apply for practising privileges at any hospital but they may choose not to accept you if they have enough people in your specialty (quite apart from any personal factors). If you are unlucky enough not to have such a hospital and your Trust cannot accommodate you, you might need to look for premises - there is more about this in Chapter 7.

Virtual and non-geographic services

If you think about it, businesses need addresses to send things to and these days this must include email. A phone is quite useful as people do sometimes want to speak to you. So how can you achieve this when you start out? Let's take things one at a time.

The attractiveness, or otherwise, of using your home address varies with the specialty you are in. Perhaps more acceptable for dermatology than G.U.M? A useful way for many is to get a PO (Post Office) Box. This can be literally a place where you collect mail or it can redirect to a geographic address. Costs have gone up recently but it is still a relatively cheap way to get a pseudo professional address. Be aware though that the underlying 'real' address is not secret and people can find it out. When you start out you can create stationery on your computer with this address and it can also be used for invoices.

When you register as a sole trader you can trade as any name you like. It could be simply your professional name or you could use some combination of your name and terms such as consultancy, services, practice or the like. It makes sense to link this to an available internet domain name and to purchase this in as many iterations as you think reasonable, e.g. .co.uk, .com, .biz, .info etc. One you will use to promote your business, the others will 'point' there to minimise confusion (and prevent its use) should someone else want to use the same name.

When you start you may just want to have some very basic details on one page; later you may want some more detail. If you can afford it, get a good designer. 'Real businesses' take money to set up; you may have little when you start so you can upgrade as you go along. Either way you can use the forwarding function of any domain name to create a professional email address; enquiries@drbloggs.co.uk rather than joebloggs@virgin.net. If you use this method you will need to ensure outgoing emails come from the same 'alias'. It might also be wise to direct replies there too, as later on you may move this official email to a secretary and this will ensure that 'customers' who just hit 'reply' on an old email in order to reach you get directed to the right person. Alternatively (and frankly much more simply, once set up), for a small fee, you can create this address in its own right based on the domain provider's URL (uniform resource locator).

Next consider getting a computerised phone number. A number of different companies provide these services (see the Webography for an example of such a company). You can get a local number or a non-geographic one which, in the early days can simply be routed to your phone. Later you can direct it to other numbers (e.g. your assistant) or a computerised switchboard. But by having the same number throughout you will not lose custom later on as returning or referred 'customers' lose track of you.

Get a second number with this and it can be used as a 'fax to email' number via the same company. Although fax, per se, is a rapidly aging technology, people (especially solicitors – who are generally quite conservative) still seem to expect it and it saves them having to scan documents at their end. Your phone can automatically be directed to voicemail if you are not available and this will be forwarded to you as an email with a MP3 file attached which you can listen to.

Lastly, if you are doing medico-legal work I strongly recommend getting a DX address if there is a local outlet – often your nearest solicitor will point you in the right direction. DX (Document Exchange) is an alternative postal system much beloved of solicitors because they are not charged by weight and they love sending you bulky packages! Get a DX address and they will not only love you but understand that you mean business!

In this chapter we have covered the issue of finding somewhere to see patients and/or clients. We also discussed the various ways in which you can make yourself available to be contacted with minimal expense in the early days. Having a full range of methods, which are 'portable', causes less loss of custom later on, as you expand.

Chapter 8 – Using your own premises

In this chapter we will look at the practicalities of having your own premises and the various financial and regulatory issues which follow from this.

The majority of doctors who start out in private or medico-legal practice will utilise other peoples' premises. This will either be a private hospital or, in some areas where private practice is organised by groups of consultants, they may buy into an existing consortium's arrangement. Even those consultants who expand their practice will often remain within a private hospital, where they may be given help if their business needs match those of the hospital. If this applies to you, you may skip this chapter.

However for some specialties and for some consultants at various points in their careers, it may be necessary to consider buying, or more likely leasing, their own premises. Surgeons are always going to need hospitals and very few surgeons indeed are likely to create their own, but all consultants need places to see people and having several different bases can obviously be advantageous.

Some specialties, like dermatology, psychiatry and paediatrics may well be able to function well with minimal hospital involvement, though my view is that it is always helpful to have a hospital somewhere in the mix. My own practice negotiated an association with our local psychiatric hospital which I think is mutually beneficial (always the best business arrangement). Even though I have not yet had to admit to them, I have the security of knowing I can access beds and they get my services on a number of committees.

If you are doing purely medico-legal work you can use any building designated for office use. However if you do any clinical work whatsoever, you will need to do it in premises which have D1 planning permission. This category, interestingly, covers health, nursery, religious, museum, art displays and public use. Sometimes developers apply for this to make their offices more attractive to a broader range of potential occupiers. It also means that setting up rooms in an old chapel, for example, may obviate the need to apply for planning permission.

Renting

In some areas it is possible to rent rooms from a landlord in a multi-occupancy building and if you can find one of these it is likely to be quite straightforward and, indeed, you may be able to do so on an ad hoc basis. There are places which routinely advertise in the BMJ, in London and Liverpool, amongst other places.

Leasing

Most people lease premises. There are a number of reasons for this, foremost amongst them being the flexibility this brings; a close second would be the cost of buying! Leasing a business property is not dissimilar to leasing a flat or house. Agents advertise, you view, you lease, usually using a solicitor to handle the lease document and perform due diligence searches etc. If you are brave and the wording does not change too much, renewals could be done without a solicitor.

Leases are usually for fixed periods, and unless there is provision for rent review within this time within the lease, the rent is fixed. It is possible to get out of leases by mutual consent or by arranging to pass the lease on to another party, with permission of your landlord. However it is best not to assume this can happen and you can negotiate the length of the lease in many cases. This will depend on market conditions to some extent. It is possible to try out a property with a 2 year lease, for example, before going for a longer lease. The downside is the rent increase which is likely to occur between the two.

Properties do not need to be freestanding. Many places lease rooms within multi-occupancy buildings. My own rooms are exactly like this and I have to say that I very much enjoy sharing a building with, amongst others, an estate agency, a bike shop, a nursing agency and a surveyor. The fact that we are next door to a very pleasant bakery and in a parade of shops which includes a local supermarket and a pharmacy all makes for a very congenial working environment. Of course having plenty of free parking space works well for patients and clients too!

Rates

The rateable value of a property is set by the Valuation Office Agency (VOA) and your local Council then charges you rates based on a set percentage of this which changes year on year.

However there is currently a small business exemption – I shan't give you figures because these are always changing – but under a certain office area you pay less – or even nothing – depending on the whim of government and the state of the economy. You have to apply to the Council for this. The level is set so that most doctor leasing, say a reception area with one or two consulting rooms, would qualify.

Apply for planning permission

The first thing to bear in mind is that you do not have to be occupying (leasing or owning the property) in order to get preplanning advice or apply for planning permission on it. Once the property is available for purchase or rent and you have an interest in so doing you can explore the planning situation. Clearly it is sensible to be 'up front' with the landlord or their agent about this so they can 'cut you some slack' to prevent someone else rushing in and buying/leasing the property whilst you are in the midst of your application.

It is probably wise, before selecting an area, to get some feel of how easy it is to get planning permission for D1 usage, if you possibly can. If you cannot, once you have 'selected' a property there is usually a process whereby you can apply (for a modest fee) to get the advice of a planning officer on the likely chances of the Planning Committee approving an application. Like any good report it usually bangs on for a couple of pages and then somewhere buried within it gives you some indication within the range 'snowball's chance in hell' to 'easy-peasy lemon-squeezy'. Depending on your attitude to risk you can then make the actual application. These days this is mostly done online and the good news (I can tell you from experience) is that if you make a mistake in the somewhat onerous process, they simply tell you and you can have another go.

As soon as you submit a successful application one of those yellow planning notices will appear on the premises and all your (potential) neighbours will get a letter informing them of your application. It is, therefore, as well to have a plan for meeting and greeting said neighbours to see if they have any objections – esoteric or otherwise. As you can well imagine, psychiatrists are pretty scary beasts, so when I applied I made sure I reassured everyone but I have to say that they were all perfectly friendly and no objections were raised!

The process usually takes a month or so and once granted you can either proceed with your lease purchase or, if you have already leased the premises (as I did because I was already seeing medico-legal clients there) proceed to the next steps.

Insurance

Of course one of these is making sure you have adequate insurance. As you will find out in Chapter 9, if you employ people you will need insurance and this may well be combined with the other two types you need if you have premises, namely public liability and contents insurance (make sure your landlord is responsible for building insurance – this is usually the case)

The Care Quality Commission (CQC)

If you have your own premises it is almost certainly the case that your will need to be governed by the Care Quality Commission. I qualify my statement because these things are not static and their rules can be somewhat difficult to understand. In fact I found myself getting very confused because they sent back something I had submitted and then told me that they could not explain what I had done wrong but that it was up to me to work out! Their descriptions of what doctors do are less than clear (to me at least) and it is inevitable that as time goes on then will seek to govern more and more people.

At the time of writing it seems that doctors working at least one session in the NHS are 'immune' from having to register in their own right merely by virtue of working privately but, as soon as you 'run an establishment' you have to register it and be its manager. So the take home message is that if you have your won premises you must engage with the CQC to establish what is required. Sadly if you have to do this there is an initial somewhat hefty fee to pay as well as a similar yearly one.

You can then expect a visit at any time! Hopefully you will keep things pretty ship shape but you would be lucky to have got everything right first time. They will appear (probably only one person) unannounced and ask to examine your policies, look at your notes, interview your staff and a patient or two – either in person or by phone – and will want to see your personnel files and examine your premises. They will ask searching questions about how you dispose of your sharps and other health and safety issues. So be prepared at all times!

In this chapter we have looked at the issues which arise for people who have their own premises, particularly for private practice. This has covered renting, leasing, rates, planning permission, insurance and regulation by the CQC.

Business for Medics

Chapter 9 - Getting paid

In this chapter we will look at the practicalities of getting paid. If you have no overheads, any money you earn is just 'nice to have'. But we all have one big overhead and it is called tax. In general terms you are taxed on what you charge rather than what you have in the bank (and especially so if what you had in your bank has already been spent!), so you had better be sure you have it before the tax bill comes in, if for no other purpose. Once you start expanding, though, you will have more overheads and sometimes paying the bills seems to be all the business is about. So starting off in a professional way and as you mean to go on, is a good idea and makes for a much more balanced relationship between your professional work as a doctor and your need for money as a business person.

Invoicing

One of the most basic things about any service business, such as we are engaged in, is having a transparent invoicing system. This starts with letting people know the basis on which they will be charged and ends with the invoicing system you use. It does not have to be anything more than a simple word processing programme when you start, though clever accounts packages exist – some quite inexpensive.

This may come as a huge surprise to some of my colleagues, but actually numbering your bills matters! Why? Well, if the taxman decides to audit you they will want to know that you have a system in place to which they can easily relate. If your invoices do not seem to have any rhyme or reason to them and, for example, they see a large gap between July and September (assuming, always, that you actually date them) they may not so easily accept your story that you were away sunning yourself in the Canaries.

On the other hand if invoices are sequentially numbered and you have long fallow periods they can be much more reassured that you know what you are doing and can account clearly for those gaps. You don't have to have any particularly sophisticated system but there must be transparency. Just as you conduct your clinical practice with one eye over your shoulder for the GMC, so it must be with your business practice and HMRC. Keep good records, and if they are electronic make sure they are adequately backed up either electronically or with good, old-fashioned, paper.

Accounts function

Your business needs an 'accounts function'. In the early days it may be you; later it could be a general factotum or a bookkeeper/accounts manager/debt-chaser. But it is important to separate this from clinical or professional matters. Sooner or later you will be faced with a non-paying patient or solicitor and you need to be able to distinguish this from your duty to the patient or the court. There is no room for emotion here. If you decide to start doing this yourself, have a low threshold for delegating it later as it is easy to do it badly and then discover suddenly that you have no money and you are really not of the right temperament (many doctors aren't) to 'chase' people.

Getting money out of people

There are some truths which are eternal. Getting money up front is extremely important. Although getting a credit card machine is associated with some onerous rules and regulations, the company which supplies them can hold your hand as you fill in the wordy yearly questionnaires. But they are really worth their weight in gold (beware, though, you need to have at least some money coming in before you are allowed one!).

This is good for (non-insured) private patients – immediately after they have seen you, I would suggest.

Getting money in the bank (good practice dictates that this should be a separate client account) before they are seen (by whatever means) is also advisable for medico-legal self-payers (and we can expect more of these in the future with legal aid cuts). This is because, once they have seen your report they may feel less inclined to pay. By adopting this approach you not only ensure payment but also distance yourself from any idea that your (independent) report is written favourably in order to please your 'customer'.

Solicitors, as a rule, have no respect for the timescales you might put for payment on your invoices. The sooner you accept this, the better. Years of experience have taught me that the only way to get money out of some of them (of course not all) is to chase them till Kingdom come. Where you are not constrained by the legal aid system, try and build this into your pricing structure. In other words acknowledge that chasing a debt of £100 may, in a certain percentage of cases, cost you an hour of employees' time plus a year's worth of interest at 8% above the base rate (this is the amount that, theoretically at least, you have the right to charge under the

Late Payment of Commercial Debts (Interest) Act 1998 and charge slightly more accordingly. At the very least, use this as an aide memoire to review your fees, annually – no-one thanks you for hiking up your fees by enormous amounts after 5 years of stasis.

Of course this is easier said than done but you see where I am going with this. Debt-chasing is a business cost and there is no point tying yourself into knots about it. Some people give discounts for early payment – you may like this idea. Alternatively, like many others, you may accept that early payers subsidise late payers just as cash payers will effectively have to subsidise credit card payers (as it is unusual for professionals to charge extra fees for using credit cards). You have to be willing to set your rates accordingly.

Another idea along the same lines is factoring; businesses exist which will 'buy' your debt for about 75% of its value and pay you 'up front'. This is only applicable to a narrow range of work – classically personal injury reports. But if you do a lot of these for solicitors (as opposed to agencies – who themselves exist on exactly this system – which is why they seem to always be going out of business) it may be worth considering.

I have also come across enterprising solicitors who invite you to up your hourly rate by, say 20% in exchange for being paid at the end of the case which might be many years down the line. As long as you do not only do this sort of work, it is something you could consider as 'part of the mix'. But do beware of this sort of work mounting up as you will recall that you have to pay tax on what you charge, not what you have been paid.

Managing the relationship

At the end of the day, putting aside ethics and good professional practice, your patient or solicitor is your customer, and, as such, your bread and butter. Now we all can think of examples of solicitors who are so egregious in their failure to pay that you really do not want an on-going relationship with them. But the vast majority are probably too preoccupied with their professional role and are not that good at running their businesses. They may be good solicitors but bad businessmen. You have to make choices. Chasing is fine but at the end of the day you may have no (sensible) choice but to (at least threaten to) take legal action.

The practicalities of this can be found on the Money Claim Online website (see Webography at the end of this book). If you are considering doing this my recommendation is to fill in the form (called an MCOL) and send them a covering letter with a copy giving them 7 days to pay or the MCOL will be issued. Then, if they do not pay, issue it forthwith! 90% of solicitors will pay when faced with a summons – the other 10% are about to go bankrupt in which case you would not be doing business with them in future anyway.

In fact because, in a significant number of cases, imminent bankruptcy is an important reason for solicitors not paying, getting in early with your claim makes total sense as once a solicitor has gone bankrupt getting money out of them can be a complex and longwinded process and you may never see your money. If this happens to you, at least you can 'write it off' as 'bad debt' on your yearly accounts. Sadly all this talk of suing is a reflection of the times – if I had been writing this book 5 years ago it would not have featured so strongly in my thinking. But recessions are a regular part of the world in which we live and several will come around in the lifetimes of most readers. During recessions businesses fail – it is an evolutionary effect – the fittest survive. Solicitors (and doctors) are by no means immune.

This happens less frequently with patients – particularly if you 'train' them to pay immediately after being seen, but you have to be much more careful. It is, of course, easier if you have stopped seeing someone; but not, perhaps, if you have reason to believe that they are not well – for example if you have been treating them for a chronic illness. In these circumstances I suggest you have a very low threshold for contacting your defence organisation before proceeding as the issues to be weighed up are more subtle.

Most patients and many solicitors pay on time but in the middle are all those people who take so many person-hours of chasing. What to do? Well, the answer is, assuming you have taken my advice above, that you just have to live with the tension. You need them and they need you. It's a bit like a dysfunctional marriage really. Sometimes you say enough is enough but most of the time you trudge on together. My experience suggests that it is most often due to inefficiency, particularly common in some smaller solicitors' offices. Sometimes they get a new person in who sorts it out and at other times they overpay you for one bill which you can deduct from the next one (one only wishes this happened more often!).

When you go to courses about getting paid they are always very aggressive about this sort of thing. However, in real life this rarely pays and it is better to be patient and forgiving and to keep their custom and good will – in most cases at least.

In this chapter we have covered the basics of tax compliant invoicing, the importance of building in the costs of debt recovery and the various ways in which late payments can be mitigated or addressed. It was emphasised that having an 'accounts function' separate from your professional or clinical function is a healthy way to approach your work. Finally we discussed the tension between getting paid and maintaining a good relationship with your customers.

Chapter 10 - Employing people

In this chapter we will look at the correct way to go about employing people, which you will inevitably have to do if you want to expand your business. As well as the general rules for employment we will consider the types of help you may need and how not to fall foul of employment or equality legislation.

Employment and other laws

It is alarming how many doctors, who are otherwise law-abiding, delude themselves when it comes to employing people. Paying 'cash-in-hand', is almost certainly going to be unlawful in all but the most exceptional of cases (and I am not even going to go there) and we, as doctors, cannot afford to break the law, so here is how to do it:

Firstly, unless the employee is on a prescribed list of close relatives, if you employ anyone you have to have Employers' Liability Insurance. No ifs, no buts; it is laid out clearly in the Employers' Liability (Compulsory Insurance) Act 1969. It can usually be bought cheaply with Public Liability Insurance and is often combined with premises insurance (useful if you have any).

Next, it is perfectly acceptable to employ anyone without a formal interview or competitive process (though we shall return to this below). Thus, asking your **NHS** secretary if s/he would like to work for you – as long as it is out of **NHS** hours – is fine. I hope you will be paying him or her considerably above the minimum wage (might I suggest something commensurate with what s/he might earn in the **NHS**?) so I shan't dwell on that bit of legislation other than to mention its existence!

The easiest (and most would argue these days, the only sensible) way to employ people is to utilise the payroll function attached to many accountants' practices. This is because it is fiendishly complicated and hemmed in by all sorts of rules and regulations which seem to change every 5 minutes. They usually charge very reasonable rates and take the headache away from you. When you start they will explain that you need formal contracts as well as disciplinary and grievance procedures to be given to each employee (we will consider what else you need when you get more than 5 employees later).

They can help you design these and you can then duplicate them with alterations for any subsequent employees. You do not have to employ people for any specific time period; theoretically you can have finite contracts. But if your problem is just the scarcity of work in the first few years then zero-hours contracts are a good solution. Work done is effectively 'overtime' but be aware that these workers are entitled to holiday pay based on the average time they have worked in the preceding 3 months.

Once you set things up with payroll, all the other headaches you might have had disappear. So, for example your employee is likely to have a *liability* to pay tax and National Insurance but the *responsibility* to pay it is yours as the employer. Worry not; your friendly payroll department will issue you with a monthly bill to pay to HMRC!

But just before you get your employee to sign the contract, bear in mind the future. Equality and immigration legislation means that you have to treat all potential employees equally, as well as checking that they are entitled to work in the UK. Whilst this may seem nonsensical if it seems evident to you that the person is British, born and bred, trust me that you are better playing by the rules from the off.

So ask your potential employee to bring you their passport. If it is a UK one, photocopy the page with their picture on *in black and white*. Apparently, according to the exact letter of the law (which is often quoted to you if you try and get a copy of your passport in a commercial outlet) making a colour copy may, conceivably, be interpreted as creating a document which could be used as a forgery.

Then file it in their personnel file – which you have (of course) just created and which will later contain their contract, any appraisals and any training they do! If it is not a UK one or they don't have a passport, immediately take advice from your payroll team before signing them up. You will also need to make sure the payroll people get your prospective employee's date of birth, national insurance number and appropriate tax paperwork – either a P45 or a P46 usually. They will let you know though!

Apart from a secretary/general factotum, who might you need to employ? Depending where you are in your business expansion you may need a bookkeeper/accounts person/debt chaser or a receptionist. If you do a lot of reports you may wish to employ someone to proof-read them (I do). Sometimes the same person can do all these tasks, sometimes not. It is important not to force people into roles they do not relish – they rarely do them well!

Advertising and interviewing

You may need to advertise. If so and you have taken part in interviewing in the NHS, you will have some concept as to how to conduct interviews fairly. If not, here are the basic rules:

Start with a written job description and a person specification – it is a good idea to have these anyway even if you do not advertise. You can advertise by any means you see fit. We got a receptionist from a free advert in Tesco's whilst our accounts manager came through an ad in the paper.

Use objective criteria to shortlist – compare people against your person spec and note where they fall short. Keep all documentation! Arrange interviews in a formal and professional manner – ideally have two people interviewing so you can compare notes and have a witness if things go very 'pear-shaped' later. Consider not only speaking to applicants but also giving them tasks. We once interviewed someone who was fine to talk to but when we gave her a simulated phone-answering task, ran out of the door at the mention of the word psychiatrist!

Don't be rushed into a decision but make it on the basis of objective criteria – still keeping all the paperwork. If you have asked for references, the job offer should be made conditionally, subject to these being satisfactory.

Managing your employee(s)

Your responsibilities do not stop once you have employed someone. Though perhaps in a less bureaucratic way, many of the things which you are familiar with from the NHS workplace still need to occur for your employees. At some level you need to have some form of risk assessment process which enables you to decide whether further checks are required.

In the absence of any requirement for patient/client contact (e.g. a typist who works at home) you may decide that a DBS (Disclosure and Barring Service - previous known as CRB - Criminal Records Bureau) check is not necessary but otherwise, I suggest you may be well-advised to have one. You may ask for forms from elsewhere but, if necessary, there are companies which can assist you to do your own checks (See Webography). If you sign up with one of these companies you will have to have your own ex-offender policy. As with any other policy you can research what others do on the internet. Even were it not a requirement it is a good idea to have one and to combine it with a risk assessment, which you have thought through, suitable for your practice. What will you do if, when you do an enhanced DBS check – necessary for working with children and vulnerable adults, you find that a prospective employee has a 'spent' conviction for theft? Your response has to be proportionate, remember.

Appraisals are a good idea – you sometimes find out some interesting things and they demonstrate that you are taking an ongoing interest in your employees' welfare. You can use forms from elsewhere (subject to any copyright issues) or design your own. Safeguarding children and vulnerable adult training is something you should consider for all staff in contact with patients or clients. Certainly these sorts of things will feature should you ever be regulated by the CQC. Appraisals do not have to be onerous but you should allocate an hour or so a year to sit down and review things. Always allow your employees to give their views. You may find something out!

Before too long legislation will require you to contribute to your employees' pensions; your payroll department will advise you when this starts to apply to small businesses but you could choose to do this already if you wish to and your payroll department can advise you about tax efficient ways of doing this, for example through 'salary sacrifice'.

Lastly you may need to dismiss someone – for example if your business contracts or you want to retire. Always seek guidance if there are contentious issues. The notice period will be part of their contract and may be longer for people who have been there some while. Always consider very carefully and, where possible, agree this on an amicable basis. But do not delay making a decision. Businesses naturally expand and contract and if you do not contract accordingly if your revenue decreases, you may find yourself in the same unfortunate position as that solicitor you were suing in Chapter 8!

If your circumstances change and you do not need to employ a person in a particular function anymore it may be that you can make them redundant. Again you should take advice (e.g. from your payroll department or a Citizens Advice Bureau) if someone has been with you for longer than 2 years, as statutory redundancy pay may need to be paid and there has to be a proper consultation beforehand with written notification.

A similar thing would apply in the unfortunate event that you had to dismiss someone for failing to do their job adequately where informal and/or formal warnings might be required; you will need to be guided as to the correct actions to take along the way (e.g. from your payroll department, a Citizens Advice Bureau or even an employment lawyer). Thankfully this is not a common occurrence.

In this chapter we have covered the basic law applying to employing people as well as the practicalities of getting the 'correct' employee in place and, if necessary dismissing them. We have also looked at the training and support which you need to provide for your employees whilst they are with you.

Chapter 11 - Keeping going

In this chapter we shall look briefly at some of the ongoing issues you need to consider once your practice is up and running.

Cashflow

Perhaps one of the most scary things about running your own business is maintaining adequate cashflow. Until you start you may be forgiven for thinking that you will simply make a profit, pocket it (you may remember from an earlier chapter to save some for tax and a pension) and enjoying life. Unfortunately life is not always that simple and there can be quite hairy times when you struggle to have enough money to pay your bills and the salaries of any employees. If you have money from another source, such as the NHS pay, you may well find yourself having to subsidise your business. It is therefore important not to 'run before you can walk' and build up your business at a steady pace so that you have adequate resources.

In the early days particularly you may not be able to enjoy your money, then, as you may need it for those months when the cash is not coming in. You will have to decide how much money, for example, you can throw at staff chasing your debts, versus your own time, which is free (to you at least) and this is why zero hours contracts can be so helpful for the small business (if the politicians allow us to keep them)

Overdrafts

Once you have your business account(s) and have been running them for a while, you should have no problem getting a small overdraft just by asking. Some banks, of course, will allow you to have one from the off but it is unlikely to be of any substance. If you really need to argue for a bigger overdraft you will need a business plan arguing what you need and why. As an example, I made a case for an overdraft equal to my monthly 'break even rate'. This is the amount of money I need to earn in order to pay one twelfth of my annual outgoings. Realistically you are only really going to know how much this is after your first year in business though.

Incidentally, although many banks give a year or so without bank charges, these will start to mount up, with or without overdrafts, so make sure to tot these up at the end of your accounting year and offset them against tax.

Loans

Most businesses need to get loans at some point. Rates are usually a bit higher than personal loans. Sometimes if you have multiple things going on in your life you can fudge the issue. For example if you have enough money for a holiday but need to buy a piece of vital equipment for your practice of roughly equivalent worth, you can apply, hand on heart, for a personal loan and use your savings to buy the equipment.

Otherwise, though, you will need to address things in a business-like way and make a business case to your bank for a business loan for the equipment you need. Of course the advantage of this method, which needs to be off set against the cheaper loan rate mentioned above, is that interest on a business loan is an expense which can be offset against tax.

A credit card machine

Once you have been going for a year or so you may be able to consider getting a credit card machine. These are usually leased from companies who then use a third party bank to process the money before it is put into your bank a few days later. Both companies take their cut and there are really complex questionnaires to be filled in every year – but the leasing company should be able to talk you through these 'compliance' requirements – they are easier if you don't sell online – which most doctors don't do.

When you apply for a machine – fixed terminals (ethernet or phone line) are cheaper than mobile ones – you will need to be able to 'guarantee' a minimum yearly income, a proportion of which will pass through the machine. In my case, from memory (a few years ago, now) the yearly income requirement was £12,000 and the amount though the machine was two thirds of this. Unsurprisingly, the people who are 'selling' this product want you as customers so they will bend over backwards to make this work. I know that when I did it I was being hopelessly optimistic but within a year or so I comfortably met the requirements and no-one complained. The lease is usually for 3 or 4 years so I don't know what would happened if you did not process enough money in the middle of the lease period. Sometimes you have to have faith though!

An accountant

Aha; if you were reading Chapter 2 carefully, you should have known this bit was coming. As it says in the learning objectives for this book 'a good accountant is worth their weight in gold'. The operative word is good. Taking my friend's father's advice I got myself an accountant the day I decided to set up in business, but it was not until many years later that I got a good one. So why are good accountants so important? Well, the short answer is that I don't know, because I am not an accountant and I have one to make up for my deficit of knowledge in the accounting field.

The slightly longer answer is that when things are going along fairly smoothly, you may not notice your accountant doing very much. Sure, it is helpful to have someone to throw your yearly figures at to crunch and give to the taxman but it is when something unexpected, like a tax investigation happens that you really need to have them onside. But, second only to my medical defence organisation, whom I have an increasingly low threshold for ringing as I grow older and, hopefully, wiser, I ring my accountant for all sorts of advice which comes up as I go along.

But here's one example of how accountants can be really, really helpful. If you earn lots of money, you need to pay lots of tax – generally. But what if your partner/spouse isn't earning any/much? Creative accountancy has become a euphemism for illegal accountancy, but in its purest (and legal) form it refers to creative solutions for problems just like these. In my case, after some discussion, the creation of a partnership seemed the right way to go, but the rules surrounding this meant that I needed a lot of accountancy support but I saved a lot of money through listening to my accountant's advice!

Your staff

We have talked about the beginnings and ends of employing people, and I have made passing reference to appraising them, but it is important, particularly as you expand (see Chapter 11) that you take good care of your staff. Depending on how many you have you can delegate this to the most senior – perhaps a Practice Manager, and the like. You or they can do yearly appraisals – you can find some good templates online, borrow one from your Trust, or make one up.

Consider, also, what training they need – both for CQC purposes and for personal development. Soon you will also have to pay them pensions – your payroll department will advise you about his. Make sure their risk assessments are up to date. How often will you check their DBS? Will you take advantage of the new DBS – updating service which allows them to register once and pay a small yearly fee to allow employers to check them from time to time – indeed will you pay that yearly fee (currently £13) for them?

Be kind to your staff. They look after you after all. You should review their pay yearly, a pay rise is nice if you can afford it and they will be grateful. Say some kind words - by email if they are distance workers - we have typists, proof-readers and a debt-chaser. If they leave after many years' sterling service, buy them a present. Give them vouchers at Christmas. Be aware that both these latter actions have tax implications so pass them by your payroll department who will explain how you can pay their tax for them. We have an annual Christmas meal to which all staff and associates are invited. The Practice pays and it is a good chance for people to meet – some may never have met before. Meals bought for employees (but not your colleagues who are just associates of your practice) are tax deductible.

In this chapter we have looked at some of the practicalities of continuing on in practice, from financial matters such as overdrafts, loans and credit card machines, through to accountants and your staff. Running a business is a job on its own and one you should take pride in doing well.

Chapter 12 - Expanding

In this chapter we will look at how you get from being someone who does the odd report or sees the odd private patient to someone who has a thriving and hopefully growing practice. Obviously the degree to which you aspire to this depends on what stage of your career you are at, but the principles remain similar. We will also consider what extra laws and regulations come into play as you grow.

How to get more work

There is little doubt that the best way to get more work is by recommendation. Hence, being good at what you do is not only good ethically and clinically but also, possibly, your strongest business tool. And being good encompasses the classic 'As' of private and medico-legal practice: ability, affability and availability. To which I might add administration (which may be delegated).

Hopefully you are already able and will get more so by continually reviewing your CPD needs and training for your expanding role. Hopefully you can be pleasant to patients, colleagues and solicitors (or, in the latter case, find someone to act as your 'front' who can be) so let us think a bit more about availability. In medico-legal work solicitors sometimes find they need an expert to confirm their availability during a court case; if you have a system which enables you or your assistant to answer the phone then and there you are more likely to be instructed. In private practice, if you can promise an appointment that week, you are more likely to get GPs referring to you and patients recommending you. A lot of this is about two things: appropriate delegation and time management.

Another way in which to get more work is by 'putting yourself about'. Networking, giving talks to GPs (if you are a specialist) and lawyers, being available for free informal advice, writing articles for 'trade journals' and giving lectures are all examples. Much of this has been covered already in Chapter 4.

Remember that the GMC rules allow you to promote yourself in an equitable and ethical manner. They do not allow you to make claims that you are somehow unique or better than other colleagues. Make sure you understand your professional boundaries in this regard before you put together any promotional material – have another look at Chapter 4 if you have forgotten this bit.

Lastly, if you find yourself getting busier - do something about it. If your waiting lists simply get longer and longer you will be in danger of losing your 'edge' and people may stop instructing or referring to you. At this point you have three constructive choices:

1. Change your work pattern, e.g. drop NHS sessions, though this is not only easier said than done but hard to reverse if things go 'pear-shaped' in your business.

2. Take on 'help' either in the form of staff, if relevant, or colleagues. The colleagues could be another person who does whatever you do but also consider ancillary staff – an ENT surgeon may work with an audiologist, for example.

3. Make arrangements to send work elsewhere (if you really don't want to do anymore).

Legal aspects of expanding

As you start to employ more people you will find that your administration gets more complex and there is a need for more policies and procedures. For example if you have more than 5 employees you may need to have access to a stakeholder pension for them. Before too long you will need to pay all your employees pensions contributions. Similarly you may need to have a driving policy (even if no-one has to drive for work). Your payroll provider, an IFA or your accountant (because by now you will certainly need one!) can usually advise you about these matters.

If you work in many specialties you should consider whether you need child and/or vulnerable adult safeguarding policies. If you cease doing NHS work and practise privately you will need to be regulated by the CQC and they may well require that you have them. In this regard, as already mentioned, take care to check the up to date situation as generally regulation increases over time. Check the CQC website with regard to the requirements of both individuals and practices to register with the CQC. Data protection/information security and risk assessment/health and safety policies are also things you should have.

If you do medico-legal work and your income crosses the VAT (value added tax) threshold (see the HMRC website for up to date information on what this threshold is) you will need to register for VAT and charge it on all qualifying bills. Your accountant can advise you further but this may be the point at which you feel the need to delegate more of your accounts function as doing quarterly returns for VAT can be time consuming.

Professional consequences of ceasing NHS work

In order to continue to practise as a doctor, you need regular appraisals and revalidation. At the point that you sever your links with the NHS, unless you work for another managed organisation you will have to make your own arrangements. If you only do medico-legal work, whilst the GMC does not require you to have a licence to practise, the medical defence organisations have said that they do and probably by the time you read this all the courts, tribunals and professional panels who instruct you will also (effectively or actually) require it.

This means that, if you are not aligned with a private hospital, you will have to make a decision about how you get your appraisals and who your responsible officer (RO) will be. You have several choices. The Independent Doctors Federation (IDF) is for doctors of all hues and your appraiser may or may not from your own specialty and the Doctors Appraisal

Consultancy can help with advice on both appraisal and revalidation. If you are registered with a locum agency (except in Northern Ireland) they can act as your designated body and provide you with RO services. Of all else fails, the GMC has a system of 'Suitable Persons' which may be worth exploring depending on your circumstances (see Webography for all of these).

Teaming up

Working on your own, with maybe one or two employees can be fun but can also be difficult. If you are considering increasing the amount of work you do there are a number of different models of working you could consider. The first is to work with others in a loose structure. This makes sense if you want to increase the range of services you offer. For example, if you are a breast surgeon and are referred a bowel problem, instead of turning away the referral you can simply say that this is the province of your colleague Mr X and make arrangements (with the consent of all parties) for the patient or client to be seen by this colleague.

The referrer does not need to know your business relationship with Mr X, who might simply be a colleague practising separately at a different address. Alternatively, especially if you have premises, you might want to rent Mr X a room or charge a fixed fee or a percentage of the fee they charge the patient (not to mention Mr Y the orthopod). Both these models are forms of association and do not constitute a legal entity. It is important that any associate is free to work for others or independently so as not to create a situation of de facto employment. Employing doctors or therapists is not generally a useful way forward in the early stages, fraught as it is with the sort of responsibility which requires you to insure or indemnify yourself vicariously on their behalf. Mutual benefit is the name of the game.

If you have one or more colleague(s) who want to take business risks with you, or a spouse/partner who earns little or no money elsewhere, you may consider forming some sort of partnership, either a simple one or a limited liability one (LLP). The pros and cons depend on your circumstances and are outside the scope of this book but you should *always take advice*, initially from your accountant but probably also from a solicitor.

Some doctors form companies. There are different types, such as the traditional limited company (Ltd) or a community interest company (CIC); again, *these decisions require careful advice*. A key issue is the different taxation structure of a company, but this does not suit everybody's circumstances. These structures all have their pros and cons. The obvious downside with a company is that whilst its profits are taxed at a lower rate, as soon as you take money out (to spend) you will be taxed at your normal rate. Perhaps this type of structure might suit someone who does not need money now but would like it later when they are not earning so much from other employment. But *never take advice about such matters from the author of a 'self-help' book!* Consult a professional, because at different times and for different circumstances the advice will almost certainly differ.

In this chapter we have covered some of the ways in which you can increase your practice, particularly the importance of personal recommendations. We have discussed some of the legal and regulatory requirements you have to comply with, particularly if you have left the NHS entirely. Lastly we looked at some of the various legal entities which you can use to team up with people.

Chapter 13 - Succession planning

Nothing lasts forever – and this includes your career. Put better, it makes sense to think of your working life as consisting of different stages. Furthermore, people have different philosophies and ideas about what makes for a pleasant life. Some want to give up work altogether at a single point in time – retirement pure and simple. Many others will be reading this book because they have nominally retired from the NHS but wish to pursue other avenues. But none of us can go on forever and it is a matter of probity that we should think ahead and not leave our patients or 'customers' in the lurch. Although it may be painful to think about it, winding down in one shape or form is necessary for us all - failure to plan ahead may lead to an abrupt or messy end to a career - which is not desirable.

At the professional level this consists of deciding what you will *not* be doing next month and/or next year. If you are doing medico-legal work you may decide, at relatively short notice, not to take on new work. From a professional viewpoint this is fine but, as we shall see below, from a business point of view there are better ways of handling this. However there are always addenda reports, court appearances and follow-up reports to be considered so it is important to plan ahead so that if you do 'pull the plug' and become non-contactable, it will not be at a time when you are most likely to be needed.

Similarly with private patients; you may wish to slowly wind down, discharging people and not taking on any new referrals, but there may well be some people whom you think should receive ongoing care – albeit not from yourself.

However, the big issue is not a professional one but a business one. What doctors often do not realise is that what they do may have value to others. Realistically medical practices are not generally going to be bought up by hedge funds but a practice, which by all accounts can take eight years to build up, may well have value to other doctors. However, even before we talk about this it may be worth your while *taking advice* on whether, within the time you are still working, you sell your own business to a company. And by this I mean a company owned by yourself (maybe with others). This is because if there is value in the business, there may be tax benefits in so doing. And these tax benefits are likely to maximised if the value of the business is enhanced by the income brought in by others.

Which is why succession planning starts early. Knowing what I just told you, you may decide that there is value to be had in working with colleagues. If, over ten years you have earned x and your colleagues have earned y, the value of the business if sold to a company (yours or someone else's) may be a multiple of y. Whilst it may well include an element of x, it is likely to be y which matters more. But please, I reiterate, *don't take my word for it*. If this book prompts you to book an appointment with your accountant this will be no bad thing.

Whether or not you decide to adopt the model of working with others for this reason, you may well decide to hand over some or part of your practice anyway. Whilst these may well start as professionals reasons - patients who need continuing support and care - if you think far enough ahead and can find someone who understands the commercial benefits of a 'going concern' there may well be several different ways to get value out of your years of hard-earned effort.

At the simplest level, if your (probably younger) colleague were to start up a practice tomorrow s/he might earn a small amount, but by working with you (who by now will have a more impressive yearly income) s/he will ally her or himself with a 'brand' which has perceived ongoing value. One way of 'monetising' this if you think far enough ahead is to give your practice a name which can outlive your time in it. Dr Jones' Practice sounds fine for when Dr Jones is around but people might be disappointed to hear that they will be seen by Dr Smith. However, if you give your practice a neutral name or add the word 'Associates' you keep your options open. Furthermore, if it is always understood by the outside world that the practice has more than one practitioner, when you eventually decide to step aside or reduce your workload, the work can go on with nary a hiccup.

This is worth money in anyone's book and all that remains is to find some way to make it pay. This is the bit where you need to take some advice from at least an accountant and maybe a solicitor but anything which has value must have a price and thus all that remains is to find the correct legal vehicle for realising this. And there are various ways of doing this. One general way, which may be attractive to both the outgoing and the incoming principal, is to have some sort of arrangement whereby the person who will be retiring in the future hands over the reins slowly. This provides stability for the business, reassurance for the incoming principal and comfort (and money) for the outgoing one. Of course any business situation where everyone is happy is all to the good.

If all this seems obvious to you it is possibly because you have direct or indirect experience of some other industry or profession. Or have worked in another country. Or are familiar with the way NHS general practice works in the UK. The concept of specialist doctors selling an interest in their business or selling a company as an ongoing concern is relatively rare in the UK, yet as we move further away from the nationalised industry model of the NHS it is inevitable that this will become more commonplace. The classic model of selling a company would be based on a multiple of yearly income generated other than by the labour of the retiring principal. This money could be paid back over an agreed timeframe from the ongoing profits of the business and quite often part of the deal is for the retiring principal to stay on for an agreed time as a director to keep a steadying hand on the tiller. Meaning that waiting until the last minute before ceasing work is not really a very good idea!

In this chapter we have considered the ethical issues with approaching the end of your working life, thought about the value of the business you have built up and talked about the different ways in which you might hand over the work and gain value from doing this. Lastly, as with any major decision, *don't rely on a self-help book.* Take appropriate professional advice!

Chapter 14 - Putting it into practice

I hope you have enjoyed reading the book, so far. Unless you are already quite experienced, you have probably had to absorb quite a lot of new concepts and, from my experience of speaking to colleagues, I know that old habits and beliefs are sometimes quite difficult to shift and new concepts hard to assimilate. So in this chapter I am going to ask you to do a bit of work. If you are lazy you can just go on to the answers, but give it a go if you are up for the challenge. Here is a 'real life scenario' which, in my experience, is often the way in which people 'get into' private practice:

> Dr Broadbent is a consultant physician who has been in post in an NHS Trust for 2 years. He quite likes the idea of doing a bit of private practice and happens to mention this to one of his catchment area GPs at a social function. The GP says he thinks he might have one or two patients he would be happy to refer. Two weeks later Dr Broadbent is pleasantly surprised to find a private referral for a lady, Mrs Threpston, which has been sent to Sarah, his NHS secretary. Dr Broadbent asks her to set up an appointment. He suggests this should be at his office, as opposed to at the local hospital where he does his outpatient clinics.

> Sarah rings Mrs Threpston and gives her the details on the phone. She creates a slot in her filing cabinet marked 'Private Patients' and puts the referral letter in there. After he has seen the patient Dr Broadbent dictates a letter to the GP at the end of a number of others and sends the (unencrypted) digital file to Sarah via e-mail. Sarah writes the letter on the ordinary headed paper she uses. It is rather long and takes her 2 hours. She pops it into the post with all the others. Dr Broadbent also asks Sarah to request payment from Mrs Threpston, so she writes a note on plain paper asking her to please send a cheque made payable to Dr Broadbent and post it to his Trust office address. Dr Broadbent thanks Sarah and gives her a ten pound note for doing the typing.

What I would invite you to do, is to think about the above scenario and make a note of anything you feel Dr Broadbent has done incorrectly. Has he broken any laws? Are there things he could have done better? When you have finished, check below to see how well you did:

What Dr Broadbent should have done

The version below describes a 'parallel universe' where Dr Broadbent does all the correct things:

As soon as he mentions to the GP that he would like to do some private practice, Dr Broadbent realises that he needs to do something about this. He tells the GP that he will look into setting things up and will tell him if and when he is ready but asks him not to refer anyone beforehand.

He contacts Dr Anwar, his medical director and tells him he would like a review of his job plan because he would like to do some private practice. They arrange a meeting for the next week. Meanwhile he rings his defence organisation and informs them that he wants to work privately. He establishes the threshold above which he needs to pay a higher premium and agrees to let them know when this is crossed.

Dr Broadbent then goes online and registers as a data controller with the Information Commissioner's Office. He follows this up by ringing a local accountant, Mr Muir, and sets up a meeting for the next day. At this meeting, he discusses his plans with the accountant who agrees to act for him and offers the services of his payroll department. They agree that, at this stage, Dr Broadbent will be a sole trader and his accounting year will begin the next month. Mr Muir registers Dr Broadbent as self-employed with HMRC. The day after, he meets the payroll manager who works with his accountant who helps him design a contract for a zero-hours worker and a disciplinary and grievance procedure.

On Saturday, he pops into a local bank and sets up 3 business accounts, current, savings and client. As he is a sole trader, the name on the account will be 'Dr G Broadbent T/A (trading as) Dr G Broadbent Medical Practice'.

Dr Broadbent meets with Dr Anwar and explains his thoughts; he formally offers the Trust a session, which Dr Anwar graciously turns down. They then discuss where he might see patients. Dr Anwar mentions that the local general hospital, where they both work, has a private suite which rents rooms to consultants. They agree that this is an acceptable location and Dr Anwar says that as far as he is concerned if it is just the occasional referral he is quite happy for Dr Broadbent to see patients there at the beginning or end of the day, even within hours, as long as it does not interfere with his NHS work. They agree to review the job plan if the number of referrals increases to the extent that it is starting to look as if he might need a whole session. Dr Broadbent rings the suite and puts in motion the necessary paperwork to rent rooms there.

Dr Broadbent speak to Sarah to see if she might like to type his private letters and do a bit of admin for him; she agrees, so he explains she would need to do this at home which is fine with her as she has a computer. He checks with her that her computer is password protected and explains that (written or digital) patient data needs to be kept separately in password protected files. They agree the password verbally between them.

Then he orders a foot-pedal for Sarah's computer (so she can type out digital files) and a digital dictaphone for himself (making a mental note to keep the invoices for tax purposes). He asks Sarah to bring in her passport which he takes home overnight to make a black and white photocopy. He puts the copy in a file, which he locks in a cupboard in his dining room which he has set aside for his private practice papers and files. He gives Sarah's national insurance number and date of birth to his accountant's payroll department. In turn they give him a P46 for Sarah to fill in (because she is still employed by the NHS).

Sarah actually has a New Zealand passport, so Dr Broadbent contacts the payroll department to check what he needs to be looking for in terms of her work status. Unsurprisingly (since she is already working for the NHS, who should have checked this out) they are able to reassure him that she is fine to work based on the work visa in her passport, which they ask him to photocopy as well. He, therefore, emails her copies of the contract to sign, together with a useful Excel file which the payroll manager has sent him, enabling Sarah to work out any future holiday pay. The contract stipulates a zero hour contract with a rate well above the adult minimum wage which Sarah is happy with so she signs the contract and returns one copy to Dr Broadbent. The payroll manager sets Sarah up on their system, which means that they will send Dr Broadbent a payslip for her when he provides them with information about the number of hours she works each month. Dr Broadbent takes a note of Sarah's bank account details to enable him to pay her.

Dr Broadbent then goes online and downloads and fills in in an application for a PO Box based on his home address. He finds a computerised telephony company and hires two lines. One he directs to his own mobile and the other to a fax which redirects to his email. He then seeks out domain names and purchases dr-broadbent-physician.com and .co.uk. He directs enquiries@dr-broadbent-physician.com to his home email address (but makes sure that the replies go to enquiries@dr-broadbent-physician.com in case he later moves email over to a secretary) and makes a note to send outgoing emails from the same 'alias'. He directs the fax line to this email address as well. He then purchases employers liability and public liability insurance (because no insurer sold employer's liability insurance on its own). He makes sure he keeps all the invoices.

That weekend Dr Broadbent wraps a cold towel around his head and devotes his time to creating a beautiful business plan. On Monday morning, he contacts the GP and tells him he is now set up to see private patients and gives him his contact details. Two weeks later Dr Broadbent finds a referral for a Mrs Threpston in his post at home (redirected automatically from the PO Box) and emails Sarah asking her to set up an appointment at the private suite. He tells her to do this on computer-generated headed paper showing his contact details which he has created on his own computer. He also mentions that invoices will be on the same paper but must show the accounting year followed by sequential numbering.

He asks Sarah to send an appointment letter to Mrs Threpston on a template he has designed. This template gives the patient details of his charges, explains that they must be settled by cheque or cash immediately after the appointment, and mentions Dr Broadbent's responsibilities as a data controller and how her data will be used for the purposes of sending appointments and writing letters to her GP (with her consent). Dr Broadbent then goes online and buys himself a digital recorder, a pedal and earphones for Sarah's computer and some files, stamps and envelopes (remembering to keep the receipts). Next he creates a shared facility for his practice work on Google Drive. He establishes that Sarah already uses Google, so has an email address which she accesses it under. He then adds this email address to the list of people who can access the practice work facility. He explains to Sarah how this works and makes sure she can access the drive. He also tells her how to download free software for the pedal (which he has researched online). He then scans his signature for her, asking her to keep it securely on her password-protected computer at home in a password protected file and gives her the stationery he purchased.

All goes ahead as planned and he sees the patient at the private suite, establishes that she is happy for him to write to her GP and that she would like a copy of her GP's letter. After the appointment Mrs Threpston gives him a cheque (made payable to Dr G Broadbent Medical Practice) and he tells her that Sarah will issue an official 'paid' invoice. He then dictates a letter for Sarah; he uploads this to Google Drive (as a MP3 file) and emails Sarah at home to tell her it is there. Sarah accesses the drive, listens to the file, types the letter and uploads it to Google Drive as a Google document (Google documents can be edited on line and are quite useful for clinic letters – reports with a lot of formatting sometimes suffer in the conversion process so uploading [and downloading again to edit] as Word documents may be a better option). She emails Dr Broadbent to tell him it is there. He accesses the file, deletes the MP3 file, edits the letter and tells Sarah by email that it is ready to go. She pastes in his scanned signature (having loaded the software when prompted by Google) and sends the letter to the GP and a copy to the patient by post in the envelopes Dr Broadbent gave her, with a copy to Mrs Threpston, marked confidential.

At the end of the month, Sarah lets Dr Broadbent know how many hours she has worked (including any administration) and he informs the payroll manager. The payroll manager sends Dr Broadbent a note of how much tax he needs to pay HMRC the next month (as you go along this will usually be sent out a month in advance so you can be prepared) and a payslip for Sarah. He passes it on to Sarah, keeping a note of sufficient detail to allow him to set up a payment from his business bank account, which he organises for the end of the month.

Well; take a breath, this was a counsel of perfection and (even assuming I remembered everything and got everything right) very few people would get it right first time (and that includes me). Some of us found things out by trial and error over many years, but you have bought this book so deserve to be told all I have gleaned over the years. You will doubtless have realised that some things are more important than others and ideally you would not want to wait for the pressure of an actual referral being in the offing – but life often works like this. So if you missed things out when you did the exercise, does it matter?

What Dr Broadbent did wrong (and was therefore responsible for Sarah doing wrong)

Well the answer is never going to be 100% black and white but here is what I think was wrong with the original scenario:

- Whilst receiving a private referral letter at an NHS address is not a problem per se, Dr Broadbent should have set things up clearly from the start

- Dr Broadbent should not ask an NHS employee to do non-NHS work, during NHS hours

- By setting up the appointment without discussing private practice in his job plan, Dr Broadbent is potentially in breach of his own contract which requires him to offer one session of extra work to the Trust before doing any private practice

- By asking Sarah to set up a private appointment Dr Broadbent is arguably already employing Sarah. Certainly this relationship has been well established by the time he gives her the ten pound note. He has therefore:

    - Failed to check her immigration status (and treat her equitably)

    - Failed to provide her with a contract

- Failed to provide her with a disciplinary and grievance procedure

- Failed to be insured as her employer

- Failed to take *responsibility* for paying any tax she owes on her pay

- Failed to establish that he was paying her at or above the minimum wage – including establishing what age bracket she falls into for this purpose. The minimum wage changes year on year but is certainly north of £6 an hour for someone over 21 and over £5 an hour for someone between 18 and 20 (in practice it was below as Sarah is 23 and it took her two hours, you will recall)

- Failed to ensure that in future she can claim holiday pay

• It is quite possible that Dr Broadbent's office, as opposed to the local hospital where he does his outpatient clinics, does not have the D1 planning consent required to see patients so he is potentially breaching local planning law

- Sarah, in ringing Mrs Threpston, is using NHS resources and also doing private work during NHS time

- By creating a slot in her filing cabinet for 'Private Patients' not only is Sarah using NHS resources and doing private work during NHS time, but Dr Broadbent is controlling data without being registered with the Information Commissioner's Office.

- We presume that Dr Broadbent is dictating his letter on NHS equipment

- By sending an unencrypted digital file to Sarah he is arguably not taking sufficient care as a data controller (registered or not). One hopes this is not the normal practice in his Trust as they would presumably be the data controller there, but everyone has a responsibility for abiding by the principles of the Data Protection Act 1998

- Sarah, by writing the letter on ordinary headed paper and posting it via the Trust's system is using NHS resources for private work. All these examples could reasonably engage the attention of NHS Protect (a branch of the NHS Business Agency)

- By asking Sarah to request payment from Mrs Threpston after the event Dr Broadbent has missed a vital opportunity to get payment from her at the time of her appointment

- A note on plain paper might conceivably be an invoice but it is not part of a proper system, and HMRC would struggle to understand where it fitted into a broader business pattern

- By asking Mrs Threpston to send a cheque to the Trust address, Dr Broadbent is, once again, utilising NHS resources for his own private practice. Additionally there is a clear boundary issue between his business and NHS work.

Well, I hope you spotted all or most of these errors and now feel more confident in your ability to set up and run a legal, ethical and profitable psychiatric business!

Acknowledgements

I would like everyone who has contributed to the genesis of this book. Those who shall not be named include all those people whom I have observed doing things the wrong way; this was the grit in the oyster upon all which came later was founded. After putting on several of my own workshops I was invited to give talks at the Royal College of Psychiatrists and then to give workshops there also. My colleague Andy Macaulay then recommended me to write a CPD module for the Royal College of Psychiatrists but I realised that the issues did not just affect psychiatrists, hence this book.

About the author

Danny Allen started his medical life doing house jobs in Kettering. After enjoying A & E and orthopaedics he rashly decided to become an 'orthopod'. After working as an anatomy demonstrator at St Marys, he toured the British Isles, failing his primary FRCS exams in some of the most scenic places in the land. After working as a GP in Australia, he decided to train as one and almost immediately did a year of ENT, which he loved and had to tear himself away from. After a spell in medicine and paediatrics in New Zealand, he did his trainee GP year in Basingstoke, but decided to do a spot of psychiatry before becoming a GP principal. As no 6 month jobs were available, so he was invited to join the local psychiatry rotation for a year, and thus began his psychiatric career. He was a senior registrar on the Bristol rotation before taking up a consultant post in general psychiatry in High Wycombe.

In 2005, in the intellectual equivalent of a mid-life crisis, he did a master's in mental health law at Northumbria University, which he thoroughly enjoyed. Although no academic, he has written over 20 papers on a range of topics. He retired from the NHS in 2011 and worked part time for a year doing substance misuse and psychiatry in an immigration removal centre; an experience which left him with very warm feelings - for the NHS. From his time as a senior registrar, he has run a business providing medico-legal reports and, over the last decade, has worked with a group of associates to provide a comprehensive service to lawyers. He is now in private practice with a number of colleagues and continues to run his medico-legal practice.

Bibliography

Marketing for the Expert Witness. Catherine Bond and John Leppard. Bond Solon Publishing 1996

Writing Medico-Legal Reports in Civil Claims – an Essential Guide. Giles Eyre and Lynden Alexander. Professional Solutions Publications 2011

Professionals and the Courts. A Handbook for Expert Witnesses. David Carson. Venture Press 1990

The Expert Witness Marketing Book: How to Promote Your Forensic Practice in a Professional and Cost-Effective Manner. Rosalie Hamilton. Expert Communications 2003

The Little Book on Expert Witness Fees. Chris Pamplin. JS Publications 2007

The Little Book on Expert Witness Practice in the Civil Arena. Chris Pamplin. JS Publications 2007

The Little Book on Getting Started as an Expert Witness. Chris Pamplin. JS Publications 2008

The Expert Witness in Court. Catherine Bond, Mark Solon & Penny Harper. Shaw & Sons 1999

Webography

www.archivebureau.com
Digital archiving

www.gmc-uk.org/doctors/revalidation/20386.asp
Suitable persons

www.hmrc.gov.uk
Tax and business

www.idf.uk.net
Independent Doctors Federation

http://doctorsappraisal.vpweb.co.uk/
Doctors Appraisal Consultancy

www.learn.bondsolon.com
Medico-legal training

www.moneyclaim.gov.uk
Online suing

www.ddc.uk.net
DBS checking

https://drive.google.com
Google Drive

www.callagenix.com
Computerised switchboard

www.iwantgreatcare.org
Private practice rating

www.drfosterhealth.co.uk
Private practice directory

www.hootsuite.com
Social media dashboard

https://bufferapp.com
Social media dashboard

Index

accountant, 12, 27, 28, 29, 30, 31, 58, 107, 108, 114, 115, 117, 121, 122, 127, 129
accounting system, 29
accounts function, 85, 91, 115
additional income, 30
alcohol, 39
associates, 122
audiologist, 41, 113
Australia, 143
bank, 33, 83, 86, 128, 130, 134
blogging, 42
BMJ, 22, 75
Bond Solon, 19, 58, 145
bookkeeper, 85, 96
Bristol, 143
Buffer, 50
business, 2, 9, 10, 11, 12, 13, 20, 25, 26, 28, 29, 30, 31, 50, 63, 64, 65, 67, 68, 70, 71, 83, 84, 85, 87, 88, 89, 93, 96, 100, 111, 113, 116, 117, 119, 120, 121, 122, 123, 134, 138, 139, 144, 147
business card, 53, 54
business plan, 12, 33, 34, 44, 131
Care Quality Commission, 16, 22, 99, 114
Care Quality Commission (CQC), 79
cashflow, 103

chambers, 18
Citizens Advice Bureau, 101
civil procedure rules, 58
client, 21, 55, 66, 68, 71, 99
community interest company (CIC), 118
continuing professional development (CPD), 59, 111, 141
CQC. *See* Care Quality Commission
CRB. *See* Disclosure and Barring Service
credit card machine, 85, 105
cremation form, 25
Criminal Records Bureau. *See* Disclosure and Barring Service
customer, 13, 71, 86, 91, 119
D1 planning, 74, 137
data controller, 55, 127, 132, 137
Data Protection Act 1998, 138
DBS. *See* Disclosure and Barring Service
defence organisation. *See* medical defence organisation
dental hygienist, 39
dermatology, 69, 74
designer, 48, 53, 70

diabetic nurse, 41
disciplinary and grievance procedures, 94
Disclosure and Barring Service, 98, 99, 147
Disclosure and Barring Service (DBS), 109
doctor, 9, 55, 67, 115
Doctors Appraisal Consultancy, 116, 147
Dr Foster, 51
drugs, 39
DX, 71
employer, 10, 12, 61, 62, 65, 95, 131, 136
Employers' Liability (Compulsory Insurance) Act 1969, 93
employers' liability insurance., 93
employing people, 29, 30, 61, 93, 101
employment, 17, 21, 22, 28, 30, 65, 93, 117, 118
employment lawyer, 101
England, 11
ethernet, 106
factoring, 87
fax, 71, 130
forensic, 25, 62
GMC, 10, 36, 45, 53, 54, 59, 84, 112, 115
Google AdWords, 49
Google Drive, 133
Google+, 50
GP, 127, 131, 132, 133, 143
Her Majesty's Revenue and Customs. *See* HMRC
High Wycombe, 143
HMRC, 10, 28, 29, 31, 58, 84, 95, 114, 128, 133, 138
holistic, 54
HootSuite, 50
hourly rate, 88
Independent Doctors Federation (IDF), 115
Independent Financial Advisor (IFA), 58, 114
Information Commissioner, 55, 59, 127, 137
Information Commissioner's Office, 55, 127, 137
Institute of Directors, 22
interpretation, 2
invoicing system, 29, 83
job plan, 12, 61, 62, 66, 127, 128, 135
judge, 27
Kettering, 143
Late Payment of Commercial Debts (Interest) Act 1998, 87
limited company (Ltd), 117
limited liability company, 117
loans, 105, 110
Macaulay, Andy, 141
maintaining a good relationship, 91
management team, 35

MCOL. *See* Money Claim Online
meals, 109
medical defence organisation, 57, 59, 90, 127
medical director, 9, 127
Medical Practitioners Tribunal Service (MPTS), 47
medico-legal, 9, 10, 16, 19, 23, 33, 39, 51, 57, 58, 59, 61, 62, 64, 65, 66, 67, 68, 71, 111, 112, 114, 115, 119, 144
medico-legal notes, 56
mentor, 12, 59
mission statement, 36
Money Claim Online, 89
MP3 file, 71, 133
myringotomy, 53
National Insurance, 95
New Year, 21
New Zealand, 143
NHS, 7, 10, 12, 15, 16, 18, 22, 34, 46, 61, 65, 66, 80, 94, 97, 98, 103, 113, 114, 115, 118, 119, 123, 128, 129, 130, 135, 137, 138, 143
non-geographical, 67
orthopaedic surgeon, 143
overdraft, 33, 104
P45, 96
P46, 96, 129
paediatrics, 74, 143
passport, 96, 129, 130
password-protected, 55, 132

patient, 85, 88, 91, 98, 111, 116, 129, 132
payroll, 12, 94, 95, 96, 100, 101, 114, 128, 129, 130, 133
Planning Committee, 78
planning permission, 16, 67, 74, 77, 81
PO (Post Office) Box, 69, 130
practice manager, 108
premises, 17, 57, 63, 68, 93, 117
principal, 122, 123, 143
private patient, 66
private practice, 7, 10, 15, 18, 22, 33, 58, 61, 112, 125, 127, 129, 135, 138, 144
probity, 38, 47, 61, 63, 65, 119
professional, 12, 22, 55, 67, 69, 70, 83, 85, 88, 91, 97, 112, 118, 119, 120, 124
professional activity (PA), 22
projection, 34
promotional material, 43
psychiatric nurse, 41
psychiatrist, 10, 16, 17, 19, 21, 22, 62, 83, 98, 117
psychiatry, 7, 19, 25, 74, 143, 144
public liability insurance, 93
receptionist, 96, 97
records, 12, 84
referral letter, 135

renting, 17, 18
responsible officer (RO), 115
rooms, 11, 17, 128
Royal College of Psychiatrists, 141
salary sacrifice, 100
self-employed, 26, 30, 128
senior registrar, 143, 144
services, 2, 9, 18, 64, 66, 67, 68, 69, 70, 116, 128
social media, 43
solicitor, 71, 85, 86, 88, 89, 100, 117, 122
St Marys, 143
statement of truth, 58
Sudbury, Pete, 9
supervisor, 12
SWOT, 40
tax, 8, 10, 12, 18, 27, 28, 30, 31, 38, 51, 58, 83, 88, 91, 95, 96, 100, 103, 104, 105, 107, 108, 109, 114, 120, 129, 133, 136
tax compliant, 12, 91
tax investigation insurance, 58
tax liability, 38
taxman, 26, 27, 84
trainee, 143
tribunal doctor, 21
Trust, 61, 62, 63, 65, 67, 68, 128, 135, 137, 138
URL (uniform resource locator), 70
Valuation Office Agency (VOA), 77
voice transcription technology, 65
webinar, 40
website, 33, 48, 49, 50, 53, 89, 114
workplace, 12, 98
Xmas, 21
zero hours contracts, 104

Printed in Great Britain
by Amazon